small
simple
ways

an Ignatian daybook for

healthy spiritual living

vinita hampton wright

LOYOLAPRESS.
A JESUIT MINISTRY

Chicago

LOYOLA PRESS.
A JESUIT MINISTRY

3441 N. Ashland Avenue
Chicago, Illinois 60657
(800) 621-1008
www.loyolapress.com

Scripture quotations contained herein are from the *New Revised Standard Version Bible: Catholic Edition*, copyright © 1993 and 1989 by the Division of Christian Education of the National Council of the Churches of Christ in the U.S.A. Used by permission. All rights reserved.

Quotations from the Spiritual Exercises are excerpted from *The Spiritual Exercises of St. Ignatius*, trans. Louis J. Puhl, SJ (Chicago: Loyola Press). Used by permission.

Cover art credit: S-BELOV/Shutterstock.com

ISBN: 978-0-8294-4541-1
Library of Congress Control Number: 2019943526

Printed in the United States of America.
19 20 21 22 23 24 25 26 27 28 Versa 10 9 8 7 6 5 4 3 2 1

Contents

To the Reader

Small Simple Ways is designed for your daily, forward motion.

We often have the sense that we're not moving forward—that we are not growing spiritually and developing into the people God created us to become. Sometimes we're stuck, stopped by failure or destructive habits. We might be emotionally overwhelmed or simply out of ideas.

We imagine a fresh start, a major shift within that will set us toward inner progress.

We forget, though, that God places us in a world of time, divided by months, years, decades, and eons—but also into instants, moments, hours, and days. *Days* are where we live. And our forward motion happens day by day and step by step. We grow into our God-imagined selves when we embrace this day or moment, making what might seem a minor choice or doing something that often is quite simple. Yet these simple acts and daily steps take us through profound conversion and maturity over time.

This perpetual daybook provides fifty-two weeks (Monday to Sunday) structured into four-week chapters. Each chapter has its own spiritual focus, which is a principle of spiritual growth and practice as taught by St. Ignatius of Loyola. These are not exclusively Ignatian principles; any Christian tradition recognizes and uses them, but they may have slightly different ways of talking about them. However, Ignatius's Society of Jesus (the

Jesuits) has specialized in helping people grow spiritually by focusing on these principles and developing spiritual practices related to them.

Formation: Weeks 1–4

God in All Things: Weeks 5–8

The Examen: Weeks 9–12

Gratitude: Weeks 13–16

The Two Standards: Weeks 17–20

Spiritual Freedom: Weeks 21–24

Consolation: Weeks 25–28

Desolation: Weeks 29–32

Imagination: Weeks 33–36

Emotions: Weeks 37–40

The Physical Senses: Weeks 41–44

Reflection: Weeks 45–48

Love: Weeks 49–52

The year of weeks is structured around these principles. In addition, each day connects the broader focus with an aspect of Christian character and/or action. The book cycles through these topics every two weeks:

Compassion	Gratitude
Courage	Humility
Creativity	Integrity
Discernment	Joy
Good Habits	Openness
Generosity	Wisdom

For example, Mondays will help you take an action of compassion or gratitude, Tuesdays an action of courage or humility, and so on. Every Sunday there is a prompt for resting. In this way, *Small Simple Ways* will help you practice Christian traits and actions systematically through one year. The structure may sound complicated, but really it is simple and builds upon repetition, which makes for forming good spiritual habits.

The work of bringing together focus, concept, and practice was done in the writing of this daybook. For you, the reader, the work is one short reading every day and one suggestion for action. Often, the action is simply a prayer, meditation, or exercise to help you engage with your life and the God who loves you.

Small Simple Ways proposes to do three things:

- inspire you to recognize grace and opportunity in each day;
- challenge you to take one action every day to live out your faith; and
- accompany you with encouragement, suggestions for the next step, and reminders of God's presence, mercy, and abiding love.

Grace and peace to you on this marvelous journey through another year, one day at a time!

Ignatian Focus: Formation

Our spiritual formation is the result of many factors beyond our control, such as where we were born and the events that influenced our families, cities, or faith communities. But we are also formed by intentional actions and habits. As children, some of us learned to pray regularly, and perhaps as adults we choose to continue habitual prayer. We choose the kinds of information we gather through our reading, television watching, social media consumption, and community involvement. That information can deeply influence the kind of people we become.

Moving forward, whether spiritually or in a more general sense, happens when we deal with big events and major challenges. But it happens at a more profound and lasting level through the small, daily involvements we choose. Spiritual teachers from many traditions have emphasized the importance of our habits and daily choices. The Christian saints grew into holiness through habits of prayer, humility, reflection, and service to others.

It's important to remember that our formation is not about being perfect right now but about growth in small increments. And when we fail, we simply try again to do what we intended and move past the failure. In *The Ignatian Workout*, Tim Muldoon offers this description and encouragement:

> Ignatius wrote about . . . spirituality as a practice, a regular endeavor through which we come to build our lives on the

love of God—to order our lives according to God's plan for us. Its focus, then, is not primarily ourselves but, rather, God. In naming his spiritual practices "exercises," Ignatius sought to suggest something about how we ought to approach them: as undertakings we must repeat again and again in order to progress slowly toward a goal. We can see spiritual exercises, then, as a part of regular maintenance for the soul. If we practice them, we will give ourselves the chance to know God more intimately and to know God's will for us.

All sorts of habits can become formation for us—habits as complex as multistep meditations using Scripture or as simple as drinking a glass of water every morning, slowly and with gratitude. Each one of us chooses what best benefits us here and now.

Compassion: Becoming

We think of compassion as a character trait, and we assume that some people are just naturally compassionate. But any virtue requires that we practice it until it *becomes* a trait in us, until it resides easily in our personality. How can we practice compassion, which is a deep sense of being with another person and of caring for that person's welfare?

Try this: When you see someone today—a person you know, or a total stranger—silently ask, *What is this person's struggle today?* The struggle may be apparent: a bad cold, fatigue from caring for two small children, stalled traffic when everyone is on the way to work.

Then offer this simple prayer:

Help that person through the struggle.

Courage: Name Your Fear

Courage is not the absence of fear but the willingness to keep going despite fear. A soldier fears attack by the enemy and yet moves into battle. A young woman fears that she's not ready to be a mom and yet welcomes the unplanned pregnancy and moves forward into the months of preparation.

Not all courage is so dramatic. There is undoubtedly a fear hiding in your daily life, one related to your job or your relationships or your physical health. Pause for a moment and try to identify what you fear. Can you also find the courage to choose to move into your day despite it, perhaps with a simple prayer for help?

Sometimes the best prayer for courage is this:

Don't let fear overwhelm me or hinder my ability to do whatever task I'm given.

Creativity: Raw Material

It's such a temptation to treat creativity as something extra, isn't it? When I've done all my work and taken care of my family and straightened the house or office and done my good deed for the day—then, if I have time and energy, I'll do something creative.

Humans are made in God's image, and one of the ways in which we are like God is our ability to create. We take raw materials and make wonderful things: solid business plans, flower arrangements, meals for family and friends, works of art. Creativity is inherent in our daily activities. So, as you do your work today, examine it for its raw materials. Then reflect on this thought: *What will this material become?*

Creative God, move through my ordinary tasks today, to make them beautiful.

Discernment: How Do I Discern?

Discernment does not seem to come naturally to a lot of people. We make decisions all the time based on the moment's emotion, sensory overload, pressure from others, whatever seems easiest, and so on. For major decisions, we apply more reason and search the heart a bit more, and probably ask others for advice.

Like any other personal quality or virtue, discernment can be developed through intention and practice. A first step is to look at your past decisions and ask a couple of questions:

- What factors do I rely on most when making a decision—how I feel, what makes the most sense, what is most positive financially?
- What factors do I tend *not* to include when I'm in discernment mode—intuition, spiritual aspects of the situation, advice from people I consider wise, my general direction or personal mission?

Holy Spirit, help me become more conscious of how
I make decisions.

Good Habits: Choose Your Influences

Every day I am formed. Situations, pressures within and without, and my own fears and desires shape me through conversations and mundane activities such as commuting or preparing a meal. Much of my situation is already determined; for instance, I've committed to a marriage and I'm an employee, and those two relationships will form me, day in and day out.

However, I can choose to include influences that will help shape me into the person God created me to be. I can choose daily prayer, regular conversation with people who encourage and teach me, and engagement in a community that helps me live out my faith. I can ask myself to list right now the influences I have already brought into my life that will help form me as the person I want to be.

Lord Jesus, which influence might I seek on a regular basis?

Generosity: Choose a Charity

How do we become generous? By hanging out with generous people. By remembering how others' generosity has benefited us. And by building generosity into our days and weeks.

- Choose a charity and commit to it.
- Set aside a percentage of income for your church or other faith community.
- Decide ahead of time what money or food or gift certificates to have on hand so that if a person asks for help, you can give something.

Lord Jesus, this is my plan to form generosity in my life . . .

Sunday

What will help you rest today? What task can you put aside to allow today to be a time of rest for you?

Heavenly Father, open my heart to Sabbath rest.

Gratitude: One "Thank You, Lord"

Building gratitude into the day is one simple act that can have far-reaching impact on your life. Practicing saying thank you every morning or evening (or both) will train you to notice, more and more, all the gifts that come to you.

In the morning, look at your life and choose one thing for which to say, "Thank you, Lord." In the evening, look back at the day and choose another thing for which to express true gratitude.

Today, I say thank you for . . .

Humility: Lift Up Another

A humble person recognizes who she is and who she is not. He does not overestimate his own importance; neither does he underestimate it. A humble person does not strive for honor and compliments but seeks to honor others.

One of the simplest ways to develop humility is to look for ways to lift up other people. Today at work or when going about regular tasks, notice one thing about another person that you can compliment or recognize in front of others.

Please open my eyes to others' value today.

Integrity: Who I Am

A person of integrity is congruent, outwardly manifesting who she or he truly is on the inside. Integrity requires that, first of all, I know who I am; then, that I behave according to who I am. "Who I am" evolves over time through my decisions and beliefs and personal disciplines. To develop my integrity, I pay attention to my growing self-awareness. I make choices intentionally rather than go through my day merely reacting. And I ask myself questions that help me clarify what I'm doing and why.

Today, ask one of these questions, or a question of your own, that gets at the heart of who you are and who you are becoming:

- "Is this what I truly want to do?"
- "Does this action reveal what is important to me?"
- "Am I speaking from my true self—or am I trying to protect myself or impress someone?"

Help me see more clearly who I am.

Joy: A Deep-Down Choice

Joy can be an emotional experience, but joy itself is not a mere emotion. It is the state of one's soul. Joy, like gratitude and other fundamental traits, is a posture toward life. It's also a deep-down choice. Choosing joy is not the same as pretending that you're happy. Joy is rooted in your beliefs about what it means to be alive and to be a person made in the divine image.

Choose joy this day by acknowledging that God's love is at work in the world. This can be difficult when confronted with all the work that evil is doing in the world as well. But consider this: Because God loves this universe into existence every moment, you have life, and all manner of life continues all around you. You possess the ability to read these words, to experience the weather, to be in friendship with others. You go to sleep, and then you wake up, and another day has arrived, and you are still in this world. Without God's love, everything would fall apart, would cease to be.

If this is a particularly tough day for you to experience joy, try to move your mind and heart back to this fact of your basic existence. If you can appreciate, even for a few moments, that you are alive and that the world is here, you have known joy.

I am here. I am alive. May I find joy in this reality.

Openness: Open on Purpose

Most of the time, becoming "open" or receptive is thrust upon us by situations that stretch us and take us outside our comfort zones. We are invited to openness when we must work with colleagues of different backgrounds, personality types, or ethnicities. We are invited to openness when we travel to other countries and cultures, or when a different sort of person enters our family through marriage or friendship.

We can become open, however, before we're under pressure to do so. I can invite a colleague to lunch or coffee to get to know her better so that my heart will open more willingly to her differentness from me. When I travel to a new city or country, I can focus on learning rather than judging and complaining about how different things are from my home country. Or, in my own home, by myself, I can read a book or magazine that expresses a political or religious view that differs from my own.

God, I choose an open stance toward you and toward others today.

Wisdom: Take a Proverb with You

The book of Proverbs in the Old Testament is a collection of wise sayings. Some are grouped according to theme, but there isn't usually a narrative to follow. Some of these wise sayings don't give us instruction but rather state what we often take to be a universal truth: "The wealth of the rich is their fortress; / The poverty of the poor is their ruin" (10:15).

The ancient sayings from this Jewish (and Christian) wisdom literature can benefit us even though they do not lend themselves to Bible study the way Gospel stories or the letters of the apostles do. One simple practice is this: Pick a chapter or part of a chapter in Proverbs and read through the sayings. When one of them makes an impression on you, stay with it.

Take note of that wisdom in your phone or other digital device, or write it down on a slip of paper or sticky note. Keep the saying with you all day, returning to it from time to time. Figure out ways of practicing the wisdom.

For instance: "Whoever belittles another lacks sense, / but an intelligent person remains silent" (11:12). It may be that this is the day you will be tempted to really slam someone through sarcasm or talk behind his back to coworkers. But if you've been glancing at this proverb throughout the day, you may just change course.

Show me, Holy Spirit, the wisdom that will help me today.

Sunday

Give yourself time to savor memories of a wise person you've known. Maybe it's your grandma or grandpa, or a teacher or neighbor.

Holy Spirit, please guide my thoughts and meditations this day.

Compassion: At the Core

The LORD is merciful and gracious,
slow to anger and abounding in steadfast love. . . .
As a father has compassion for his children,
so the LORD has compassion for those who fear him.
For he knows how we were made;
he remembers that we are dust.
—Psalm 103:8, 13–14

Compassion lies at the core of God's character. Jesus' life and teachings demonstrate this. Compassion can be a focal point for us as, day by day, we form our character as followers of Jesus.

Consider a conversation or other interaction you might have today. If you make compassion your goal, what will your part of that interaction look like?

Form in me, Lord, your compassionate heart.

Courage: "Prompt and Diligent"

[In prayer] I will ask for the grace I desire. Here it will be to ask of our Lord the grace not to be deaf to His call, but prompt and diligent to accomplish His most holy will.
—*The Spiritual Exercises* (SE) 91

Ignatius of Loyola was a soldier as a young man, and soldiers are trained to follow the will of their superiors—and to do so promptly and with diligence. It's not surprising that Ignatius would use such language to describe his desires as a Christian. He applied this concept of discipline and loyalty to his spiritual life.

We pay a price for becoming slow and lax in our work for God's kingdom here on earth—that is, in the part we are designed to play in the divine plan. We waste time deciding again and again to follow holiness rather than remaining firm in our initial decision to do so. We waste energy by doing our tasks half-heartedly and half-well rather than by developing excellence in all we do. We wear ourselves out by becoming deaf to holy whispers that would prevent us from wandering in the wrong direction and having to find our way back to the best path.

Today, I review my dedication to the path I have chosen with Christ.

I want to become more responsive to your voice, because you are God of my life.

Creativity: Name Your Gift

The LORD spoke to Moses: See, I have called by name Bezalel son of
Uri son of Hur, of the tribe of Judah: and I have filled him with
divine spirit, with ability, intelligence, and knowledge in every kind
of craft, to devise artistic designs, to work in gold, silver, and bronze,
in cutting stones for setting, and in carving wood, in every kind of
craft. Moreover, I have appointed with him Oholiab son of
Ahisamach, of the tribe of Dan; and I have given skill to all the
skillful, so that they may make all that I have commanded you.
—Exodus 31:1–6

Part of our formation as spiritual people involves the gifts God has placed within each of us.

What are your gifts? Are you an artist? Good with money? An expert organizer? A personality that attracts young people into stimulating conversations? A person who has a strong but gentle way with children? The ability to teach or instruct? A knack for solving problems?

Name one gift that you recognize in yourself and bring it to God in your prayer or meditation.

God, I recognize this gift in myself: help me nurture and use
it well.

Discernment: Gradual Wisdom

Do not be conformed to this world, but be transformed by the renewing of your minds, so that you may discern what is the will of God—what is good and acceptable and perfect.
—Romans 12:2

Do a quick Internet search and you'll find many books on decision making, also known as discernment. Wouldn't it be nice if we could follow ten easy steps and make the right decision every time?

True Christian discernment, however, grows out of mind-set, purpose, and character. As we allow God to transform and renew our minds—you might call this ongoing conversion—we increasingly see our lives as God sees them. We desire the same outcomes God desires. We hunger for justice, compassion, healing, and holiness. This is the gradual growth of wisdom. All of this guides our decision making.

God who continues to renew me in every way, please assist me as I discern about [blank]. I trust you to lead me when there are still so many gaps in my understanding and character.

Good Habits: Whatever Happens

And not only that, but we also boast in our sufferings, knowing that
suffering produces endurance, and endurance produces character, and
character produces hope, and hope does not disappoint us, because
God's love has been poured into our hearts through the Holy Spirit
that has been given to us.
—Romans 5:3–5

Divine love designed us with the capacity to develop character out of whatever happens to us. The teachings of parents and church have played a role in the kind of people we have become. But let's not discount all the "stuff that shouldn't have happened"—the trials and problems we have suffered and worked through year after year.

Holy Spirit, I remember going through [blank]. Help me linger
with that memory. Open my eyes and heart to whatever growth
or wisdom developed in me during that time.

Generosity: Cheerful Giving

*Each of you must give as you have made up your mind, not reluctantly
or under compulsion, for God loves a cheerful giver.*
—2 Corinthians 9:7

The apostle Paul did not assign a percentage for how much people should give financially to God's work. Paul asked churches to take up regular collections that he could then deliver to other churches that were in great need.

- People were not to be compelled to give.
- They were to make up their own minds about how much to give.
- They were to give cheerfully, not reluctantly.

Part of our formation as Christians is intentional thinking and planning in regard to our financial resources. In planning how and how much to give, we make generosity a priority. We will give not according to how we feel at the moment but rather will follow what we have chosen as a result of thought and prayer.

*God who gives every good gift to us, lead me as I form a plan
for the giving of my resources.*

Sunday

Today, your prayer can be silence.

Lord Jesus, help me go to a quiet place and find rest with you.

Gratitude: Begin with Thanks

Then he took a loaf of bread, and when he had given thanks, he broke it and gave it to them, saying, "This is my body, which is given for you. Do this in remembrance of me."
—Luke 22:19

"When he had given thanks"—sometimes we miss this phrase in our hurry to begin what has become our communion liturgy. But we should pause here. Jesus is introducing a new concept: His body is the bread and his blood the drink of this holy feast. He begins by giving thanks. In the Jewish prayer tradition that has formed Jesus, this thanksgiving is almost as natural as breathing.

What about our prayer? Do we always begin with thanks? I confess that my prayers often begin with my own needs or desires. I am still training myself to thank God for the gifts of my life before moving on to a list of requests.

Begin your prayer with one of the following:

Thank you, God, for watching over my life and remaining present to me.
Thank you, Lord, for your mercy, which is new every morning.
Thank you, Holy Spirit, for helping me pray when I struggle to do it.

Humility: Walk with Jesus

"Come to me, all you that are weary and are carrying heavy burdens, and I will give you rest. Take my yoke upon you, and learn from me; for I am gentle and humble in heart, and you will find rest for your souls. For my yoke is easy, and my burden is light."
—Matthew 11:28–30

How can I grow in humility? By learning from Jesus. By spending time in Jesus' company. By walking beside Jesus through the Gospel stories.

Jesus, help me walk with you this day, and please accompany me and train my heart to grow in humility.

Integrity: Just Yes or No

> *"Let your word be 'Yes, Yes' or 'No, No'; anything more than this comes from the evil one."*
> —Matthew 5:37

Jesus understood that the more we talk, the less clear we can become. If we can't say something simply, then perhaps we should reconsider what we are trying to say.

When my explanations go on and on, what is happening? Am I trying to justify my words or behavior? Have I become argumentative, trying to pressure someone to agree with me? Or am I avoiding my true explanation, to which the listener might not be receptive?

It can take a long time to form the practice of communicating clearly. We are surrounded by half truths and constant "spin" in the way people or companies represent themselves. We are accustomed to relentless sales pitches and exaggeration. If we answer people simply, as Jesus suggests, we might even be considered blunt or unfriendly.

> *Jesus, show me how to do this—to speak simply and with integrity. Help me see my own habits of communication that need to change.*

Joy: The Path of God's Presence

You show me the path of life.
In your presence there is fullness of joy;
in your right hand are pleasures forevermore.
—Psalm 16:11

The human inclination is to search for joy before anything else. This psalm shows us that joy comes to us as we walk the "path of life," the path that brings us into God's presence.

God, what is the path of life in my situation right now? Help me search for your presence first of all, trusting that the joy will come.

Openness: Postures of Prayer

When you pray today, try this experiment:

- Say a simple prayer while sitting down.
- Say it again, standing up.
- Say it again while standing, with both arms down at your sides and your hands in fists.
- Say it one more time, only now extend your arms in front of you and open your hands, palms up.

Now reflect for a moment. How did your different postures affect the way this prayer felt for you? Was it difficult to open your hands? Did that make you feel vulnerable? If it did, that might be a clue that you struggle to trust God, or that you want to hold on to something, which feels easier to do when you make a fist.

Kneeling, standing, lying down, bowing—none of these postures does anything for God. However, they do have an impact on us. If you make it a practice to open your hands during prayer, the movement itself might help your soul trust a little more. A physical posture of openness can help us *become* more open. And every moment in which we open even a tiny bit more toward God's presence—that moment is profound progress.

*God, even when I don't feel like opening my life to you, I do
want to welcome you.*

Wisdom: Something to Love

Wisdom is radiant and unfading,
and she is easily discerned by those who love her,
and is found by those who seek her.
—Wisdom 6:12

I'm convinced that if we spend a lot of time around wise people, we will be attracted to wisdom more and more. And, growing to love wisdom, we will recognize it easily when we encounter it.

In seeking wisdom, begin by seeking the company of people who possess it. They may be friends or teachers. They may also be writers or leaders you have never met except through books or documentaries. As Christians, we believe in the communion of saints—the "cloud of witnesses" mentioned in the book of Hebrews. Although they no longer live on this earth, they accompany us in spirit, and their lives continue to instruct us through the stories we know about them or the words they have left to us.

Make a habit of finding wise people—whether someone you know personally or the saint whose biography sits on your bookshelf. It's never too late to make wise friends.

Who are the people I know who demonstrate wisdom? Bring us together, Lord, so that I can learn from their example.

Sunday

What can you do every Sunday to let go of busyness? A few suggestions—but please, choose just one. Don't try to "accomplish" the whole list:

- Turn off your phone, at least for a few hours.
- Ignore the desk with bills, notices, and so forth.
- Choose not to go shopping.
- Choose not to cook a big meal; perhaps do that on Saturday and have leftovers on Sunday.
- Refuse to do home repair unless there's an emergency.

May I be gentle with myself today and with the loved ones who are with me.

Ignatian Focus: God in All Things

They should practice the seeking of God's presence in all things, in their conversations, their walks, in all that they see, taste, hear, understand, in all their actions, since His Divine Majesty is truly in all things by His presence, power, and essence. This kind of meditation, which finds God our Lord in all things, is easier than raising oneself to the consideration of divine truths which are more abstract.
—*The Letters of St. Ignatius of Loyola*, William J. Young, SJ

The concept of "God in all things" is more countercultural in the realm of Christian religion than it might initially seem. If we believe that God is present in all things, then we cannot believe, simultaneously, that the world—and all the people in it—are fundamentally wicked. The theological concept of "God in all things" begins with creation, not with the Fall. We acknowledge that sin and evil exist in this world and are active, but we trust that what made God declare, "It is good" about every aspect of creation remains true. God seeks us—and Jesus came to us—to bring our lives back into alignment with this truth.

Thus, people who believe that God's "presence, power, and essence" operate throughout creation do not have countless reasons to fear other people, other cultures, or new information unveiled by scientific discovery. God is at work in every thing and in every person—to the extent that each one of us is open and responsive.

Furthermore, "God in all things" theology is confident that every human being houses the deep and abiding desire to be in relationship with God. Sometimes that desire is buried so deeply that it can take a lifetime for a person to discover it. But we assume that God's created loved ones long for the Creator. Saint Ignatius taught, prayed with, and gave spiritual direction to people because of his belief that the Creator was already at work in their lives and had, in various ways, already gifted them with graces—even though people might not yet understand or have words for those graces.

When we embrace the truth of "God in all things," we expand our experiences of God, encountering divine love and purpose in the here and now.

Compassion: In All People

We practice compassion when we acknowledge that God is not only "in all things" but also in all people. Every person is made in God's image.

This is easier to see in some people than in others. Most of us express our divine mark by helping others, speaking respectfully, showing tenderness to our children, or working conscientiously at our jobs. It is sometimes hard, though, to recognize the work of God in others. Perhaps we see that a person has corrupted the divine impulse to help others into the need to control them. The speech that can be used for good also has the power to abuse—thus, some of the most articulate people are also the cruelest. Even love for family and friends can be corrupted into neediness and manipulation.

So, if you are trying to show compassion to someone who is difficult to like (and harder to love), try to identify divine traits in that person through their "corrupted" expressions. You will see that every person is indeed made in God's image. Recognizing that is the beginning of true compassion.

Lord, you know I have trouble getting along with [blank].
Help me see, in this person, your divine image.

Courage: Grace in Any Situation

If you believe that God is in all things, then you will find the courage to dwell in any situation with grace. You can make that court appearance, knowing that God will be there. You can sit with your dying friend because God is there, too. You can go to work today because you trust that God will be acting through the flawed people and dysfunctional systems we sometimes encounter there.

Where do you need courage? Bring to mind circumstances today that call for courage. Now, where do you think God will be present? If you can't imagine where, then ask for the grace to see it. And take courage.

Lord, you know the situation I'm facing. Help me see you there.

Creativity: More Possibilities

Because God is in all things, every moment of your life contains more possibilities than you can perceive. Because God is creative and has made you creative, you can count on there being more options than what are now apparent.

We think of creativity as a quality we apply to writing or painting or building. But creativity is required most in daily situations, especially those that are going badly. Creativity can help us see a better way. Creativity opens our eyes and minds to the options that at first seem nonexistent.

Do you feel that you're up against a wall today? Do you feel trapped, unable to solve a problem, out of ideas? Pray for the ability to see with God's eyes and to perceive your life with God's creative mind. There will be a way. God is present. And you are full of more solutions and fresh ideas than you now imagine.

Discernment: Ripe with Information

Every thought, emotion, physical sense, and intuition you have today is ripe with information. God designed us this way. When we attend to how we feel and what we think and notice, we are already discerning.

God is in that emotion—yes, even that uncomfortable emotion you'd rather ignore right now. That very emotion is attached to something deeper you need to pay attention to.

God is in that scent that jarred you to attention this morning, zapping you back to a beautiful childhood memory and giving you the comfort you needed. Say a prayer of thanks for it.

God is in your thought process. The Holy Spirit helps you make connections and reason your way to where you need to be.

God is in your gut reaction, too. This can be as simple as the primitive fear response that kept you from walking into traffic on your way to work. Yes, "God in all things" is that normal and mundane.

Allow yourself a few moments to remember one thing—a thought, emotion, sense, or gut reaction—that stands out for you today. Stay with that and discover what it may be telling you.

Good Habits: Noticing God's Presence

One of the most powerful habits you can form in your daily life is the act of noticing where God is present for you. This one habit will lay the groundwork for other healthy practices.

We might expect that God's presence is big or dramatic. This expectation, though, will work against our ability to recognize where God truly is. The truth? Divine love resides in your half-a-dozen sentences to your loved one as you head out into the day. It resides in your tendency to be pleasant to strangers, or to go out of your way to help a young mom get all three of her children on the bus. Divine presence hums in workplace conversations, in a colleague's noticing that you look tired or discouraged, in the afternoon coffee break that preceded a really good idea.

God is present in the ordinary because the ordinary is magnificent. The ordinary is magnificent because it springs from the love that creates us moment by moment.

Before you do another thing, locate some divine love in your ordinary activity today.

God, I see that you were present today in this way: . . .
Thank you!

Generosity: Never Completely Comfortable

I've never met a person who was completely comfortable with how she approached people in need. I'm not completely comfortable with how I approach poverty and those oppressed by it. I give to charities, including my church, which maintains various ministries to those in need. I vote for politicians whose policies address poverty and oppression. I give money or food to people on the street who ask—not always, but often.

But I can't solve all their problems. My donation will not turn around life for anybody. Some days, it seems that my charity is just a dribble of water getting absorbed in desert sand.

Is God truly in all things, including my efforts to make a difference in the world? I believe so. Generosity is the product of hope. I don't know how my donation or support is going to affect the outcome, but I do know that it matters. I do believe that God's love is active when I am generous in ways large and small.

What generosity can you practice today? Look for one way to give, and trust that it will matter.

Jesus, please accompany my attempt at generosity today.

Sunday

Allow yourself to take a nap today. Because of all the stress we carry and all the strange hours we keep, most of us do not rest enough. Life will wait while you acquire some restorative sleep.

God my creator, grant restorative rest to my body and mind today.

Gratitude: It Is a Choice

I have always struggled to accept the life I have as opposed to the life I wanted. Some matters just didn't turn out as I'd hoped. And I'm not talking about small matters, such as where I got to go on vacation. My dashed hopes were bigger and more permanent.

I've discovered, through years of struggling with loss and disappointment—which all of us must do—that gratitude truly is a choice. In fact, seeing God in all things is also a choice. Is God in the life I ended up with? If I answer yes, then it follows that I am grateful for this life.

In saying that "God in all things" applies to my life, I'm not claiming that God planned what happened or how things turned out. God does not manipulate our lives. I have free choice. And every person whose life has touched mine also has had free choice. Some of the outcomes in my life have had more to do with my own choices, and some outcomes were influenced more by others' words, actions, and choices. Yet, God's presence is a constant. And *that* is what I'm grateful for. Some days I can be grateful for outcomes, but I don't think God expects us to be happy about everything that has happened. God wants us to be grateful that we live in holy love.

Even if you do not feel that gratitude is among your strongest points these days, can you thank God that your life is constantly held in divine love?

Humility: My Life and Everyone Else's

How can I be humble today? By acknowledging that God is present not only in my life but also in everyone else's:

- The driver who is texting while driving in front of me? God is present in his life.
- The woman who is screaming at her kid in the grocery store? God is in her life, too.
- The unkempt young man who is too high to make sense yet keeps trying to talk to me? God is with him.
- The group of "mean girls" hanging out in the coffee shop, talking loudly about their latest victim? God remains with them, waiting for any chance to draw them nearer.

God's love is not all about me and everyone I consider a decent, productive person.

When you see someone today who strikes you as vulgar or unpleasant or a lost cause, say to yourself, "God is intensely interested in this person and pays close attention to every detail of her life." That is, in itself, a powerful prayer.

Integrity: The Real You

When you understand and believe that God is present in your real life, you'll find it easier to live with integrity.

When you reject who you are and try to be someone else, you embark on a path of pretending. And you'll discover that it's difficult to feel connected with the divine. God is with the real you, not the pretend you.

Therefore, ask God to help you see your true self and God's presence—God's image, qualities, desires—in that true self. This is the path to integrity and truer friendship with God.

God, you know all about the pretend "me." Help me put that person aside today.

Joy: God and Joy

When we receive the images and sensations and thoughts of God that come to us, we can dwell in life with more ease. Also, we can find joy more often and in more situations.

This also works in the other direction: when we encounter joy, we can more easily encounter God in that same place.

So, where do you see hints of the divine on this day? With the divine beside you, joy is possible.

What has given you joy on this day? Can you see beyond that joy to its Source?

> *God, here is where I found—or where I hope to find—joy today.*

Openness: Welcome God

Recognizing God in all things leads quite naturally to openness in your heart.

If you see God in a person of another culture or ethnicity, how could you ever be able to close your heart to that person?

If you see God in an expression of art that is unfamiliar to you, how could you possibly dismiss that art as inferior or unimportant?

If you see God in the person whose political opinion you do not share, wouldn't you be more willing to listen to that different viewpoint?

Sometimes we try to be open, but it's too difficult. If that's the case for you today, then change your strategy. Ask God to reveal the divine spark in whatever or whomever you cannot be open to. You may not be able to welcome an idea or a personality, but you have welcomed God time and time again. Welcoming God can be the first step to welcoming other people.

I open my heart to you, God, however you are present in this person. Help me recognize you.

Wisdom: God's Mind Coming to Us

Wisdom enlarges understanding and sharpens viewpoints. Wisdom discerns between similar options. Wisdom builds a memory of examples to help guide us.

Wisdom is God's mind coming to us in tiny increments that we can comprehend. In fact, wisdom itself is fine evidence of God-with-us.

You may not feel close to God right now. But can you savor the wisdom stored up in your life? The wisdom that has soaked into your way of thinking and acting is one manifestation of God that is quite active in you. And close to you—so close, it has become your own mind thinking.

I acknowledge, God, that you have already nurtured wisdom in me. Help me see it.

Sunday

Today, turn to Psalm 23—in your Bible, online, however you can—and read through it at least twice. Sit with the words and allow them to soak into your thoughts and feelings.

God who loves my soul, please embrace me with calm and hope.

Compassion: Sheep without a Shepherd

When he saw the crowds, he had compassion for them, because they were harassed and helpless, like sheep without a shepherd.
—Matthew 9:36

When Jesus saw the crowds, he saw their need. They were like sheep without a shepherd—meaning they could not fulfill their own needs but instead waited for someone who could.

We are created to love God and for God to love us. Therefore, our need for love is not a failure on our part—and it is not a sin. It is poignant evidence of our identity and purpose: to live in union with our Creator.

Notice that when Jesus saw the crowds, he was not "disgusted with them, because they were selfish and sinful, like people who didn't know how to behave." Honestly, though, that might be my first response, especially on days when I deal with crowds of people in a large city when the weather is messy and the trains are running late. Some days I look at other human beings and the last thing I feel is compassion.

Brother Jesus, you showed us how to see others and how to think about and act toward them. Forgive my failure at compassion. Help me see others as you do.

Courage: What Frightens You?

Daniel was a young Hebrew carried away into exile by one of Israel's enemy nations. Because he was young and strong—and therefore seen as useful—he received extensive education and training in the foreign land, where the God of Israel was not honored. Yet, Daniel continued praying to God, believing that God was still present in that place. Daniel's faith in God's presence gave him courage when he was thrown into the lions' den for not worshipping the king. An angel of God then saved him from the lions.

Whether we believe this really happened or read it as a legend used to teach the Israelites about God's protective power, we can learn from the story. Do we believe that God is always present to us? If so, how does that influence how we react to frightening events?

What frightens you these days? Try to name that fear and pray something like this:

God, help me trust that you are with me. This fear is with me, too. I pray that your presence will become as real to me as this thing I fear.

Creativity: Begin with What's There

*When the wine gave out, the mother of Jesus said to him, "They have
no wine." . . . Jesus said to them, "Fill the jars with water." And they
filled them up to the brim. He said to them, "Now draw some out,
and take it to the chief steward." So they took it. When the steward
tasted the water that had become wine, and did not know where it
came from (though the servants who had drawn the water knew), the
steward called the bridegroom and said to him, "Everyone serves the
good wine first, and then the inferior wine after the guests have
become drunk. But you have kept the good wine until now."*
—John 2:3, 7–10

We don't create something out of thin air; we begin with what we
have. Could Jesus have simply made jars of wine appear at the
wedding? We assume that he could have provided wine however he
chose. He chose to take what was present—water—and create wine
from that. On another occasion, when he fed thousands of people,
he began with five loaves and two fishes that were on hand.

We can find encouragement in these examples of Jesus'
"creative" work. Like him, we can begin with what we have. What
the Holy Spirit guides us to do with it—that's the creative part.

What is your creative work, and what do you have to
start with?

*Lord Jesus, show me what I already have; may I work with you
to create what that material will become.*

Discernment: In the Search

We are quick to recognize God's presence in our answer to a problem or when we find clarity for a decision. What we are not so quick to see is God's presence while we are searching and asking:

- Sometimes, growing wise and patient while trying to solve a problem is more important than finding the solution.
- Sometimes, waiting for clarity is what brings us clarity.
- Sometimes, discovering God's company in the darkness is what we need more than a light to help us see in the darkness.

If you are in the middle of trying to find an answer or make a decision, try some version of this prayer:

God who loves me, I know that you remain with me when I don't know what to do. You are here when I can't figure out a solution. You are here while I struggle to make the right decision. You are here, wherever I am on the continuum of discovery. Thank you.

Good Habits: Choose Your Sources

Finally, beloved, whatever is true, whatever is honorable, whatever is
just, whatever is pure, whatever is pleasing, whatever is commendable,
if there is any excellence and if there is anything worthy of praise,
think about these things.
—Philippians 4:8

We find the qualities of Philippians 4:8 in the company of people who exemplify those qualities. We find them in Scripture readings or in worship, in certain books or films or other art forms, in physical work or athletic excellence. Where we find these qualities, we find God.

God appears in places where we don't always expect to find God, and also in places where we are sure to encounter divine presence. Surrounding ourselves with what is true, honorable, pure, just, pleasing, commendable, and excellent is a fitting habit to develop. What do you consider pure or just or true? What sources of these qualities are in your life now—or could be?

Dear God, I want these qualities in my life, but I'm not always
careful to seek them. Show me one source today for something
commendable, pure, worthy of praise.

Generosity: Our Response to God's Abundance

"Give, and it will be given to you. A good measure, pressed down, shaken together, running over, will be put into your lap; for the measure you give will be the measure you get back."
—Luke 6:38

Some so-called Bible teachers and evangelists of our time have twisted this Scripture verse, interpreting it to mean that the Bible provides a formula for getting rich. Things couldn't be further from the truth. In this verse, Jesus is describing a fundamental response to God's abundance. We can give generously because God gives to us generously.

God, because I believe you are always with me and your gifts to me are abundant, I seek to share those gifts generously. What gift can I give to someone today?

Sunday

"God in all things" means that God is already in
your life. Sit with this truth for a while today.

*Jesus, you said that Sabbath was made for humanity, not the
other way around. May I use this day for the benefit of my soul.*

Gratitude: Thank the Person You'll Never See Again

You're trying to get into the restaurant carrying three bags and leading a weary six-year-old by the hand. A guy is coming out as you're going in. He's on his phone, hardly notices you, and seems in a hurry. But he does see you, backs up a step, and holds the door open for you. A simple thing, but he didn't have to do it. Even though he's engaged in a phone conversation, make a point to meet his eyes and say, "Thank you."

May I notice one small kindness another does for me today—and may I remember to say thank you and mean it.

Humility: Those I Help

God is in the person I am trying to "help."

Many of us in the United States love to go on mission trips to help "the poor." We show up for a few days and build a church or dig a well. We try to converse with those we are helping. We share meals with them—which often means that we eat in their homes and they prepare meals to share with us.

Invariably, one of us helpers says something like, "I thought I was giving my energy and help to them. But they gave so much more to me." At some level, this means recognizing and admitting that God was already quite present and busy in these people and this place before we arrived. If we are wise, we allow this realization to humble us. We do not bring God to people. We don't possess God so that we can give God to anyone. But it is a temptation to fall into this way of thinking.

Lord Jesus, as I seek to help people I encounter who appear to need encouragement, support, or physical resources, please remind me that I am not the only one bearing gifts.

Integrity: Honest Questions

Now there was a Pharisee named Nicodemus, a leader of the Jews. He came to Jesus by night and said to him, "Rabbi, we know that you are a teacher who has come from God; for no one can do these signs that you do apart from the presence of God."
—John 3:1–2

Nicodemus's statement leads to the conversation we all know well: Jesus says that a person must be born again, and that God loved the world so much that he gave us his only son. We don't know how close Nicodemus was to becoming a follower of Jesus, but we see that his directness opened a door of inquiry, and Jesus was happy to meet Nicodemus there. Jesus knew that Nicodemus still had a way to go before he understood, yet he recognized that the man came with honest questions.

When we have the integrity to ask the questions that matter, Jesus will patiently enter into conversation with us.

What is your burning question?

Joy: Before We Knew

*Then [Nehemiah] said to them, "Go your way, eat the fat and drink
sweet wine and send portions of them to those for whom nothing is
prepared, for this day is holy to our LORD; and do not be grieved, for
the joy of the LORD is your strength."*
—Nehemiah 8:10

The people of Israel had been in exile for decades. When they
were finally allowed to return home and rebuild their city wall
and the temple, someone discovered scrolls containing the law of
Moses. On a specified day, all the adults stood before Ezra the
priest as he read the Law to them—it took hours. At the end of it,
many were weeping, perhaps because they feared punishment. In
their long exile, the people had forgotten God's law and had not
been keeping it. But Nehemiah comforted them with the words
of this passage. It was a day to rejoice: yes, they had been without
the Law, but they had never been without God.

You and I can rejoice this very day because—despite our
failures and forgetfulness—God continues to love us and be here
with us.

*Dear God, I rejoice now because you loved me when I didn't
even know how to follow you. In fact, your love has brought me
to this point in my life.*

Openness: Our Response to Those Doing God's Work

Whoever receives you receives me, and whoever receives me receives the one who sent me.
—Matthew 10:40

In this passage, Jesus is speaking to his disciples. Our openness to God will manifest in our openness to Jesus and to anyone who brings his message. If you wonder whether your heart is receptive to God, you might reflect on how you have responded to those who do God's work, who carry out justice, mercy, kindness, and compassion.

Show me my heart, dear God.

Wisdom: Present at Creation

Proverbs 8 presents a personification of Wisdom, who tells us this:

> *When [God] established the heavens, I was there,*
> *when he drew a circle on the face of the deep,*
> *when he made firm the skies above,*
> *when he established the fountains of the deep,*
> *when he assigned to the sea its limit,*
> *so that the waters might not transgress his command,*
> *when he marked out the foundations of the earth,*
> *then I was beside him, like a master worker;*
> *and I was daily his delight,*
> *rejoicing before him always,*
> *rejoicing in his inhabited world*
> *and delighting in the human race.*
> —Proverbs 8:27–31

Little wonder that so many people who study the created world—scientists of every kind—acquire awe and wisdom. They may or may not profess a religious faith, but their close acquaintance with creation often stimulates deep questions and a sense that this universe is more than what mathematic formulas can describe.

Stoke your wisdom and your sensitivity to holy presence by spending some time with nature.

Sunday

If you are able, and if weather permits, take a
leisurely stroll along a beautiful path: a forest trail, a
running path, the sidewalk of your own
neighborhood, a nearby park.

*Holy Spirit, please help me quiet my anxieties and fears and
rest in divine Presence.*

Ignatian Focus: The Examen

The Examen is a prayer that the Jesuits have used for centuries. It is a bedrock of Ignatian spirituality. Various forms of the prayer exist, but here is a description that makes the Examen quite accessible to anyone who decides to try it.

Ask for light.
Ask the Holy Spirit to guide your thoughts. You want to see your life as God sees it, not as you are inclined to see it—either hypercritically or not honestly enough.

Give thanks.
Look for anything in your day so far that indicates God's presence in your life. And give thanks for it. It might be as simple as a good night's sleep or as complex as a difficult conversation with your teenager that went better than expected.

Review the day.
Look back through the day and think about what happened, how it felt to you, how you responded. Notice which events or moments stand out for you—these probably deserve a little more attention.

Face your shortcomings.
Identify what you might have done differently. You made an honest mistake; you took an approach that did not work very well; you misunderstood someone else. Or, notice where you

simply did wrong. You went into that meeting expecting the worst of another person; you harbored ill will against someone; you helped spread a rumor. Face these moments and actions and bring them to God. Ask for help to do better next time. Ask for wisdom to understand how you can improve. Ask for forgiveness for sinning against another.

Look toward the day to come.
As you anticipate tomorrow—meetings, conversations, tasks, responsibilities—bring to God in prayer whatever concerns you. Ask for the help you need to face tomorrow with faith, hope, and love.

Saint Ignatius considered this prayer of thanksgiving and review so effective that it was the only one he insisted that Jesuits pray every day. Members of this religious order do not live in communities that pray together several times a day; the Jesuits have been called contemplatives in action. But the Examen prayer of thanksgiving and review is a crucial daily habit for them.

The meditations of weeks 9 through 12 will focus on reviewing various aspects of daily life. They will offer practice in using the Examen.

Compassion: Remember Specifically

When have you experienced compassion? When you were a child? A teenager? A parent to small children? Going through a midlife crisis? Try to pinpoint a specific act of compassion that graced your life during that difficult time. Remember who demonstrated this compassion to you.

Thank God for that person. Reflect on the way his or her compassion made an impression on you, how it touched you and helped you move forward.

I thank you, God, for [blank], whose compassion helped me
and continues to touch my life.

Courage: When Were You Courageous?

Today, call to mind a time when you were courageous. What did you have to face? What made the experience frightening or threatening? In what way did you act courageously despite the circumstances?

Offer a prayer of thanks for that courage. Reflect on how those moments of being courageous helped build the life you have now, and pray for the courage you will need tomorrow.

Lord, I'm not sure how I found the courage to get through that situation, but your grace was there to help me. Continue to show me how to live with courage and not with fear.

Creativity: What Did You Create Today?

This very day, you have created something. What was it?

- A beautiful thought
- A timely response to another person
- A little poem or picture
- A big plan or idea
- An activity to bring people together
- An action to bring healing

Describe in a few words your creative work this day.

The world thanks you for your creative work, and so does your Creator God.

Discernment: Pinpoint a Decision

Discernment, or making an informed decision, brings wisdom, memory, and life experience to a present set of circumstances.

For instance, during this day, you made at least one decision based on your memory of a similar situation or on the wisdom you have accumulated. Can you pinpoint a specific decision from today (even a mundane or minor one) and the memory, experience, or wisdom that you connected to it?

Pause for a few moments and savor how the Holy Spirit strings together the constant dynamics of our learning, remembering, and choosing.

Good Habits: Reflect on a Habit

You have the capacity to reflect, day after day, on the habits that shape you. For instance, you have discovered that drinking coffee later than two in the afternoon will hinder your falling asleep at night. So, you change the habit to drink decaf or some other less potent beverage past midafternoon.

Think back over the past few days, and pick out one of your habits. It could be a habit you've been intentional about, or it could be a habit you've simply fallen into. What is the habit? Can you trace the effects of it? Does it help you, or hurt you, or make little difference in your day?

Having reflected on this habit, do you see a reason to change it, let go of it, or do it more intentionally?

Generosity: Attitude Precedes Action

We place a lot of emphasis on being generous—on *doing* acts of generosity. But it can be helpful to discover what causes us to feel more generous or inspires us to generous deeds.

Try to remember times during the past week when you have felt inspired to be especially generous. What was happening, and when did you notice the inclination to be generous? Were other people involved? What did you do or say, or what did someone else do or say?

Is there a way to re-create the conditions that incline you toward generosity? Is there one small thing you can do to stoke that flame of inspiration in yourself?

Sunday

Today, put away your worries. If you have trouble with this, write them down in a list and then put the list away.

Lord Jesus, help my whole self—body, mind, spirit—express true prayer today.

Gratitude: Seven Names

In your journal or on a piece of paper, write down seven names of people for whom you thank God—one name for every day of the week. These are the people who encourage you or are kind to you. If it's been a bad week, perhaps you include your parents simply because they brought you into the world. On any day you can give thanks for strangers who helped you or were merely friendly. You can give thanks for the farmer who raised the tomatoes you bought at the grocery store. Even if you don't know someone's name, you can describe that person to God and give thanks.

Humility: See Yourself Realistically

So often, it seems that we are forced to humility by humiliation. Humiliation is a form of harm from which you must recover—another person can humiliate you by exercising power over you so that you feel less important or that you are of a lesser status. Humility is the ability to see yourself realistically and honestly. When you have humility, when you are humble, you don't see yourself as better or worse than you really are.

You can't control the kind of people who might try to humiliate you, but you can create an environment in which you become more self-aware. This means that you form relationships with people who are loving yet honest with you, people who see your gifts and recognize where you need to grow. This means that you consume information that is trustworthy and helpful and stay away from exaggeration and spin and self-serving propaganda.

What helps you see yourself more honestly? What encourages and what hinders you in this?

*Jesus, you walked this earth with humility. Please guide
me now.*

Integrity: Make Use of Bad Examples

Today, try to recall a situation in which you witnessed someone act *without* integrity. You'll remember it because it caused you pain or disappointment or anger or discomfort. What happened? What about this behavior lacked integrity? How did you respond? How did others respond? Allow yourself to feel the true effects of a person lacking integrity.

God my creator, remind me of how much it hurts others for me to be deceitful or misleading or two-faced. Help me walk with integrity as I go through this day and interact with people.

Joy: Delighting Others

Consider the people who live with you or are close to you in some other way. Focus on one person and ask yourself: When have I seen her or him joyful? What gives this person delight?

Now, do your best to bring joy to this person in the next few days. It can be small and simple, such as bringing her favorite dessert or playing his favorite music. It can be a few meaningful words: commenting on how you love her passion for her work or reminding him of the first time you heard him sing and were amazed at his beautiful voice.

You have the power to help others experience joy. Use that power with love and delight.

Openness: Savor the Capacity for Growth

At various times in your life, something in you has opened up. There was a moment when you finally understood something or admitted that you cared for someone. There was a day when you relented to God's stubborn, seeking love. There was another day when you finally let someone help you.

Recall one of those opening-up times, and allow yourself to feel those emotions and think those thoughts all over again. Savor your capacity for growth. Thank God for not giving up on your fearful, closed heart.

Wisdom: Remember a Wise Person

We've all encountered someone we consider wise. Maybe it was a grandparent, teacher, mentor, or friend.

Allow yourself a few minutes to remember this person's wisdom and the impact it has had on you.

Thank you, God, for the wise people who have added so much to my life.

Sunday

Find some colored pens or markers and write down the Lord's Prayer. Make it as artistic as you like. Use color and your own design as you meditate on each phrase.

God of the universe, may I rest in the confidence that you uphold me with the very breath of life.

Compassion: Put It on the List

I was hungry and you gave me food.
—Matthew 25:35

From time to time, I make daily lists for myself. They include tasks I need to do and errands I need to run. They also include works of mercy, because I become so involved in my own life that I forget about other people. So, on my to-do list for the day, I will write, "Do one thing for another person."

Most of us neglect caring for others not because we are mean or selfish but because we are self-absorbed and distracted. Why not put compassion on the to-do list?

Anticipate the people you will likely be with tomorrow (perhaps as part of your Examen prayer). Pray something like this:

Holy Spirit, alert me to a person to whom I can show compassion tomorrow, even if it's a simple act such as looking at someone and acknowledging him or her in a kind, attentive way.

Courage: When Was I Afraid?

As I prayerfully think over this day's events, I ask these questions:

- When, today, did I feel fear? What triggered that feeling?
- Can I put into words what I was afraid of?
- How did I respond to feeling afraid? Did I try to avoid what I feared, or did I confront it?
- Do I expect to face this same fear tomorrow?

Now, spend some time meditating on this Scripture:

> I am convinced that neither death, nor life, nor angels, nor rulers, nor things present, nor things to come, nor powers, nor height, nor depth, nor anything else in all creation, will be able to separate us from the love of God in Christ Jesus our Lord.
>
> —Romans 8:38–39

Heavenly Father, may I find courage in your love for me.

Creativity: Learn to Recognize It

When, today, did I solve a problem?

When did I devise a plan or write out a strategy?

When did I search for the best way to express an idea?

When did I come up with a story or game to entertain my children?

Creativity is a normal part of every day, but I might not see it that way unless I train myself to recognize it.

God who created me—and who designed me to be creative—open my eyes to see how I use this gift day to day. Help me embrace and celebrate this part of myself.

Discernment: Can You Trust Intuition?

As we develop a practice of discernment, we learn about intuition. Sometimes we experience a strong hunch or an underlying sense of certainty. How much can we trust those moments?

Intuition is a function of the human personality, just as imagination and reasoning are. Some people access their intuition quite naturally, but this doesn't mean that their hunches are always right. Likewise, a person who is not used to working with intuition can learn how to access it and become more comfortable trusting it.

Reflecting daily on your experience is a good starting point for more intuitive work. When you pray the Examen—the prayer that helps you review the day—you can focus on your flashes of intuition. Intuition can feel emotional, or it can come through the intellect—a sudden thought about a situation. For example, when you had that conversation, what did you feel about it, deep down? When you had to choose among three options, did you have a sense that one was the best?

Holy Spirit, I want my intuition to become part of my process for paying attention to and participating in whatever you're doing in my life. Guide me as I develop this aspect of discernment.

Good Habits: Gradual Change

Examen-like thinking can help us break bad habits. The power to reflect on past behavior might provide us with an incentive to make a change, and reviewing behavior regularly creates the opportunity for gradual, long-term change.

For instance, I had fallen into the habit of grabbing a coffee and a snack on my commute home from work. This added extra caffeine and calories that I did not need. I began to review how I had felt previous times after drinking and eating at that time of day. I knew that it dulled my appetite so that I didn't feel much like having dinner with my husband at home—but I ate dinner anyway, to be polite because he had cooked it. I also realized that I wasn't particularly hungry right after work; I simply wanted to give myself a treat after the workday.

I knew that telling myself I could *not* have an after-work treat would backfire and make me want it even more, so I gave myself permission to buy a coffee and a snack, but I chose to review that impulse every day when I left work. Sometimes I did get the drink and snack, but just as often I decided I didn't really want it.

Lord, I want to review my behavior related to [blank]. Please give me insight and the strength to develop a better routine.

Generosity: What Gets in the Way?

If you resist doing something, there's a reason for it. The resistance won't go away until you have faced the root of it. Perhaps you have noticed that something in you just resists being generous. Try looking back at times when this resistance has been strong:

- Remember an interaction in which you could have been more generous in your praise of another person. Why did you resist?

- Remember when you could have made a financial contribution but chose not to. Why? Did you feel that what little you could give would not make a difference? Did that appeal for money bring up for you the general sense of helplessness you often feel about dire needs in the world?

- Someone you don't know well needed some help, and you could have given it but resisted. Were you afraid that one request would turn into more requests?

The Examen trains us to notice what has a positive impact on us and what has a negative impact. Any feeling that arises during prayer—whether positive or negative—merits further reflection.

Lord, you and I know what generous actions I have resisted in the past few days. I need your help in looking into that resistance.

Sunday

A wonderful Examen prayer for Sunday is this:
reflect on the graces of the past week, and
savor them.

Heavenly Father, open my heart to Sabbath rest.

Gratitude: Looking Back with a Focus

Although the Examen prayer is generally used to review the day, you can review longer periods as well. When reflecting upon the past month or year or decade, it's best to choose one focus for the reflection rather than try to review every part of your life. Try to look back in gratitude for these things:

- The friendships that have been good for you
- The trials you have overcome
- The skills you have learned
- The different places in which you have lived
- The gifts and talents in yourself that you have discovered

Today, Lord, I reflect on the past [month, year, group of years] and thank you for . . .

Humility: Grasping for Status?

Our humility is often spoiled by our desire to gain a higher status. In your prayer today, try to remember a time recently when you found yourself grasping for more power:

- Why did gaining status become an issue for you?
- Were you experiencing any kind of fear, such as the fear that, if you did not gain status you would lose power over your situation?
- Were you feeling threatened by the power of another person?
- Did you feel that no one was on your side?

Bring all this to God:

I'm not sure why I was grasping for higher status in that situation, God. But I want to understand better what was going on with me. You ask me to walk in humility and to serve others rather than become powerful over them. I want to live in this way, but at times I am driven to another mind-set because I feel threatened in some way. I need your help with this.

Integrity: "Less Than" People

> *My brothers and sisters, do you with your acts of favoritism really*
> *believe in our glorious Lord Jesus Christ? For if a person with gold*
> *rings and in fine clothes comes into your assembly, and if a poor*
> *person in dirty clothes also comes in, and if you take notice of the one*
> *wearing the fine clothes and say, "Have a seat here, please," while to*
> *the one who is poor you say, "Stand there," or, "Sit at my feet," have*
> *you not made distinctions among yourselves, and become judges with*
> *evil thoughts?*
> —James 2:1–4

Today, I review the various people I have been with in the past few days: at the workplace, the grocery store, the gym, in church, and so on. And I ask myself these questions:

- Whom do I automatically see as "less than"? People who have a lower-paying job than mine? People who are overweight? People who don't dress well? People who sound uneducated when they speak?

- Did my feelings about those people cause me to treat them differently from how I treated others? For instance, did I ignore them or avoid speaking to them directly?

> *Jesus, you gave priority to the "less than" people of your day:*
> *lepers, well-known sinners, women, the poor. Forgive me for*
> *showing partiality. Show me how to do better.*

••• **THE EXAMEN / WEEK 12** •••

Joy: Profound Dependence

Rejoice in the Lord always; again I will say, Rejoice.
—Philippians 4:4

The writer of Philippians did not say, "Look on the bright side," or, "Pull yourself together." Rejoicing "in the Lord" was the key to getting through whatever happened in this young church. Such rejoicing was not naive optimism or spiritual self-sufficiency but a profound dependence on God's continuing love, comfort, wisdom, and help.

This evening, look back at your day and take joy in this: You endured, with God's help. Perhaps you did more than endure—you thrived or you grew or you succeeded. Whatever the case, rejoice.

I rejoice in you, Lord, because . . .

Openness: What Shuts Us Down

We might review the day in terms of when we were more open to people, or to God. Or, we might look at when we were the opposite of open: when we shut down.

What causes a person to shut down, to cease to be open to others?

- Fear of being rejected, judged, or criticized
- The belief that others are not listening to us or believing us
- Overwhelming emotion such as sadness, anger, or grief

Can you identify a time when you shut down, and why?

Try to bring this experience to prayer.

Wisdom: Learn from Mistakes

Even when we've been foolish, we can learn from our mistakes. A quality of wisdom is that no experience is wasted.

When have you *not* been wise recently? What mistake did you make or what foolish thing did you do or say?

Can you pinpoint where things went wrong? If you were in that situation again, what would you do differently?

Sunday

Listen to a favorite piece of music. If you have time,
listen to it more than once.

Holy Spirit, please guide my thoughts and meditations this day.

Ignatian Focus: Gratitude

Gratitude was so important to Ignatius that he believed ingratitude was the deadliest of sins. . . . [H]e wrote . . . that ingratitude was "the cause, beginning, and origin of all evils and sins." . . . Toward the end of the Spiritual Exercises, Ignatius urges us to pray for gratitude: "To ask for an intimate knowledge of the many blessings received, that filled with gratitude for all, I may in all things love and serve the Divine Majesty."
—Jim Manney, *Ignatian Spirituality A to Z*

To seek gratitude is to seek a clear vision of life. Rather than skew our mental effort toward what is wrong or difficult, we correct it to include what is good and beautiful. Gratitude is not merely the polite habit of saying thank you. It goes deeper than words, reaching into our most fundamental attitude toward others and ourselves. We can be grateful for the kindness, practical help, or comforting presence of another person. We can also be grateful for our own gifts, our ability to learn, and our unique history and personality.

Gratitude trains us to see, before everything else, all that God has done for us and given us and the ways in which God has made it possible for us to more fully express the divine image. Through gratitude, we set our every thought in the context of God's continuing love for all creation, including ourselves. When we start from an acknowledgment that God creates us and loves us, we learn over time to see that suffering is not the ultimate reality—God's love and presence are.

Ignatius saw gratitude as a practice that helped people recognize the eternal reality of God's love for humanity. He understood ingratitude as a form of rejecting God's love, of refusing to see the truth about God's majestic purposes for this world and our flourishing in it.

Do we receive this life as a gift? Do we celebrate the fact of being alive in this universe? Do we welcome others who are different from us? Do we perceive problems and troubles as raw material out of which something good can form? These questions are appropriate as we reflect on this holy quality called gratitude.

Compassion: Gratitude Nurtures Compassion

Gratitude creates an open posture toward others.

Gratitude does not look for reasons to criticize or judge others.

Gratitude appreciates the good—or the desire for good—in others.

Gratitude welcomes others' efforts, even if they fall short.

Gratitude celebrates others' growth, gifts, and distinguishing characteristics.

As we develop our gratitude, we also nurture our compassion.

God who loves us all, help me focus on one of these today:
openness, nonjudgment, appreciation, welcome, or celebration.

Courage: People We Don't Know Well

It takes some courage to leave the door open to a person we do not know well, especially if our early impressions are negative. If I have already formed an opinion of that person, the relationship will likely remain stuck (this works both ways).

One small but powerful step to take for opening doors and dissolving early judgments is to find something positive about the other person and thank him or her for it. For instance, "I'm not sure I agree with what you said about that topic, but I appreciate your willingness to speak up and be honest. Thank you." This simple expression of gratitude might lead to an entirely new conversation.

Help me become truly grateful for this person, who I don't know well.

Creativity: Weapon against Resentment

As a writer of many years, and as an editor who has worked with scores of writers, I have learned that certain attitudes can stop creativity cold. One is resentment. In any artistic field, there is the whiff of competition and tension in the air. Who will get the book contract? Whose book will sell the most copies? If we forget that, in God's economy, we have an abundance of gifts and opportunities, then we can mistakenly take on an attitude of scarcity: if that person succeeds, then I must fail.

One of the most effective weapons against resentment is daily thanksgiving. It's almost impossible to be resentful and grateful at the same time. When another writer achieves success, can I thank God that her gifts will now reach further into the world? When I struggle with self-doubt, can I thank God for giving me the desire to create that perseveres through it all?

Lord, guard my heart from resentment. Remind me to thank you for the gifts you have given others and for how those gifts make my life richer.

Discernment: Loosen That Death Grip

If you have a decision to make, begin with gratitude. Why? It shifts your posture toward God, others, and your life in general. In becoming more grateful for the life you have in this moment, you can loosen your death grip on what you want or what you're afraid of losing. Healthy discernment requires an open mind and heart. To discern well, you must be free to accept this outcome—or another one.

> *God, you have already given me so many gifts. Thank you that I'm alive and that I receive all these good things from you and from other people. I trust that however this decision works out and wherever my life goes from here, your gifts will be waiting for me there, too.*

Good Habits: The Valuable Habits

We form habits without even thinking about them, don't we? Drink a certain kind of coffee every morning; go through the same routine before bed; check the same sites online every day.

We also form habits of thought without being intentional. We make the same complaints when stuck in traffic, or replay the same despair over our bank account or today's drama at work.

Here's a challenge—form a habit because you see it as valuable:

- When you awake, say, "Thanks that I woke up—that's a good start."
- When traffic slows because of roadwork, say, "I'm glad the city actually takes care of our roads—nice to have a working infrastructure. Thank you."

These are two examples, but you decide what you need.

Generosity: Overlooked People

Be generous with thanks, especially to people who are often overlooked. Someone cleans the building you work in. Someone solves computer problems. Someone just supplied you with a hot meal on this long road trip—maybe it's fast food, but those workers filled your order. Someone delivers your mail. Someone fills your prescriptions. Someone teaches your children or grandchildren.

Who will you thank on this ordinary day for doing their ordinary work?

Sunday

Thank God that you have another day to
experience this life.

Lord Jesus, help me go to a quiet place and find rest with you.

Gratitude: Simple Thanks

Thank you, God, for [name], who encouraged me when I needed it most.

Thank you, God, for [name], who loved me enough to be honest with me.

Thank you, God, for [name], who gives me a safe place to talk about my life.

Humility: Share the Credit

The next time someone praises you for a job well done, give thanks to that person and then mention all the other people who were part of the success. Give credit where it is due. Gratitude for others' contributions will not only maintain your humility but also prevent others' skewed perceptions. Remember that the high-profile people nearly always get credit while quieter workers are overlooked.

Integrity: No Empty Praise

Avoid empty praise or thanks. People know when you're trying too hard, or even lying.

Thank people for what is true—what they really have done that you appreciate.

Guard me, Holy Spirit, from empty words.

Joy: Awaken the Joy

Gratitude and joy are best friends; you rarely experience one without the other. If you—even reluctantly—murmur a thank-you prayer, you remind your heart of something that is praiseworthy or good for your life. That reminder awakens the natural human response to good, which is joy.

Inner developments like this can be very subtle, but I encourage you to notice the good for which you can give thanks. Dare to awaken the joy that rests deep within you, waiting to be summoned.

Openness: Praying for Others

We can't always choose the people who come into our lives. We're stuck with our blood relations; we can't control who attends classes with us or becomes our coworker. If we attend a church or social organization, we will face people who irritate or frustrate us.

It can help—it truly can—to thank God specifically for people we'd rather not have around us. When we mention a person's name in prayer, something begins to happen within us. In thanking God for someone, I prepare myself to receive that person.

Dear God, this week I pray especially for [names].

Wisdom: Recognize Who Helped

A wise person understands that she has come this far in life because others have helped her and loved her. Not all of them were friends or family members; they were health-care workers, colleagues, and total strangers, all doing their part in her life.

Thank you, God, for [names], who have contributed to my life.

Sunday

Today, read Psalm 103.

May I be gentle with myself today and with the loved ones who are with me.

Compassion: Begins with Gratitude

A man—let's call him Ed—owed his employer a lot of money, and when the employer called in the debt, Ed begged for mercy. He received it and was forgiven his debt. Ed then went to another man—let's call him Calvin—who owed him a very small amount of money and demanded that he pay up. Calvin begged for mercy but did not receive it; Ed had Calvin thrown into prison for his debt.

If Ed had any sense of gratitude for the mercy shown him, he would have shown compassion to Calvin. But he evidently forgot his own begging for mercy. Perhaps Ed didn't really take responsibility for his own debt, or maybe he felt that he was entitled to such magnanimity. Either way, he saw Calvin's debt as his own fault, thinking he didn't deserve any leeway whatsoever.

Jesus tells us a story like this in the parable of the unforgiving servant. It teaches us that a lack of gratitude spreads into every part of life. It hinders the development of every other virtue.

Lord, show me when or where or with whom I have lacked a proper sense of gratitude.

Courage: Fixed in Memory

> *I waited patiently for the LORD;*
> *he inclined to me and heard my cry.*
> *He drew me up from the desolate pit,*
> *out of the miry bog,*
> *and set my feet upon a rock,*
> *making my steps secure.*
> *He put a new song in my mouth,*
> *a song of praise to our God.*
> *Many will see and fear,*
> *and put their trust in the LORD.*
> —Psalm 40:1–3

Through gratitude, we focus on what has gone well. Giving thanks for a task completed or a relationship healed fixes these events in our memory.

Memory can serve us well when it is time to face a new task or grapple with another fractured relationship. The psalmist turns an experience of God's help into a song, one that can be sung again and again, as a reminder of what God has done in the past. When the psalmist is once again in a pit and in need of rescue, the song of remembrance will be there to fuel courage.

Can you write two or three lines so that you remember God's faithfulness and help the next time you need it?

Creativity: Seeing Opportunity

When we have an outlook of gratitude, we assume that we are blessed and live in a world that is, at its core, amazing and lovely. Thus, we look for hints of blessing and loveliness in everything we experience. When our experience is harsh, we look for the opportunity to soften it. When it is cruel, we explore means of introducing mercy and kindness.

In other words, a grateful attitude affords us the flexibility to see a situation in more than one way.

Think of a situation you face, or have faced recently, that did not seem so blessed or beautiful. Try to remember the scene in detail.

If you could revisit that situation, for what could you give thanks? Can you, looking back at it, shift your view to see things differently? In what way might you introduce peace, patience, or another healing quality?

Jesus, I do remember a situation in which a basic stance of gratitude might have helped. Guide me as I think through this and pray about it. I want to use this experience to prepare myself to act differently in the future.

Discernment: The Power of Thank You

It's quite difficult to think clearly when I'm angry or resentful. Those emotions cloud my thoughts and fill my heart with a kind of noise that makes it hard to hear God's whisper. I know better than to make a decision when my interior world is in an uproar.

However, I don't always have the luxury of waiting until anger has dissipated; perhaps I need to make a judgment call by the end of the afternoon.

How do I come to a state of equilibrium? Begin by saying thanks. It won't be easy at first.

Thank you, Lord, that I have the freedom to make choices.

Thank you that you understand every detail of what's going on, including how I feel.

Thank you for [name], a person made in your image, who is not in my life by accident.

Thank you for providing wisdom.

Please calm my heart. Please still the racket in my mind.

Thank you for loving me.

Thank you for trusting me to live out my faith in this situation.

A few thank-yous can be surprisingly effective in calming the inner storm. Gratitude might shift my entire perspective.

Good Habits: Don't Forget the People at Home

You have lived with your family for decades. You know one another's quirks and weaknesses. You've had lots of fun times—and lots of heated arguments.

Don't neglect the habit of gratitude in the daily grind. There truly is a change of atmosphere in a room when someone says, "Thanks." You may have been knocking heads ten minutes ago over the family schedule or the mess in the kitchen. But then your teenager picks up his dirty sports gear from the family-room floor, and you say, "Thanks, honey."

You and your spouse take turns cooking and cleaning up. Even though you've done it this way for years, he still says, "Thank you," when you do the dishes. It still feels good to be thanked.

Thank him for letting you spend fifteen minutes alone after a stressful day.

Thank her for sorting through all the medical bills.

Thank him for working out the snag on his sister's computer.

Thank her for talking with her grandma on the phone.

Thank you communicates, "I recognize that you chose to do something good and helpful. That means a lot."

Whose day won't feel just a bit softer after that?

Generosity: Say Thanks

Bring to mind one or two people who have helped and encouraged you.

Contact one of those people today—through e-mail, a phone call, a message on social media, or a card or letter—and thank that person for enhancing your life.

It doesn't have to be a long letter or an hour on the phone. Make it brief and simple, and full of gratitude. The message will come across.

God, you have placed some wonderful people in my life. Thank you for [name]. May this thanks reach him or her at just the right time. I hope it's encouraging and gives a lift to the day.

Sunday

Have an unhurried conversation with someone you love.

God my creator, grant restorative rest to my body and mind today.

Gratitude: Enter the Gates

Enter his gates with thanksgiving, and his courts with praise! Give thanks to him, bless his name!
—Psalm 100:4

In this psalm, notice that the person giving thanks and praise does so while entering God's holy place. The same could be said for a person "entering" God's presence—that is, for a person who becomes present to God through prayer or silence. As we become more aware of God's presence with us, and as we learn to respond to God's presence with our own attention, thanksgiving and praise will become natural responses.

Gratitude—giving thanks—is a habit we cultivate intentionally, but it is not a mere matter of human will: "I *will* give thanks! I *will* be grateful!" Like any other true virtue, gratitude is ultimately our response to what God is already doing.

God, draw me into your welcoming gates, your holy courts.

Humility: Our Interdependence

Indeed, the body does not consist of one member but of many. If the foot would say, "Because I am not a hand, I do not belong to the body," that would not make it any less a part of the body. And if the ear would say, "Because I am not an eye, I do not belong to the body," that would not make it any less a part of the body. If the whole body were an eye, where would the hearing be? If the whole body were hearing, where would the sense of smell be? But as it is, God arranged the members in the body, each one of them, as he chose. If all were a single member, where would the body be? As it is, there are many members, yet one body.
—1 Corinthians 12:14–20

When you thank a person for her help, you admit that you needed help. When you thank God for the abilities you've been given, you admit that these abilities are gifts you could not give yourself.

Thus, gratitude and humility go hand in hand. A world in which thanks are exchanged among people is a world in which people recognize their interdependence.

In your prayer today, thank God for two or three people, and be specific about the gifts they bring to your community.

Integrity: Everything Is a Gift

What do you have that you did not receive? And if you received it,
why do you boast as if it were not a gift?
—1 Corinthians 4:7

One simple step toward becoming a more grateful person is to look honestly at your life and remind yourself of what Paul said to the Corinthians: everything you have is a gift—why do you act as if you should get all the credit?

Show me my gifts, Lord, and stimulate in me a response
of thanks.

Joy: Still Blessed

Ignatius invites us to look at our own history of sin and evil in light of the goodness of God. Even though we reject God, he still blesses us. The saints and angels still pray for us. The earth does not swallow us up. Rather we enjoy the bounty of God's splendid creation.
—David L. Fleming, SJ, *What Is Ignatian Spirituality?*

One day a preacher entered my commuter train car. He began his short and effective sermon with, "If you woke up today, the rest is just gravy!"

It is a blessing to breathe, to sit or stand, to lie down, to listen, to put thoughts together, to dream, to weep, to experience emotion, to have desire.

What part of your existence today do you experience as blessing?

Openness: The End Isn't Up to You

Only God could say what this new spirit
gradually forming within you will be.
Give Our Lord the benefit of believing
that his hand is leading you,
and accept the anxiety of feeling yourself
in suspense, and incomplete.
—A Prayer by Pierre Teilhard de Chardin, SJ

As the years go by, I become increasingly grateful that the end results of my life are not up to me. I gladly engage with my life each day by making choices, committing to projects, daring to dream, and so on. But I do not want the pressure of being accountable for how everything ends.

Isn't it a relief that God of the universe has gathered us into the divine family? That God's wisdom and power and love keep this universe in motion? That this same God, the king of heaven, assumes responsibility for our development as humans made in the divine image?

Today, I say a huge "Thanks!" because I can open my arms
wide, expecting to receive abundant goodness from you, the
God who loves me.

Wisdom: Seeing Large

We look at the infant who cannot yet crawl, let alone walk. But we also see, in that infant, the young woman who will run and dance. We have the ability to see ahead, to see "large"—the bigger picture, the days yet to come. Sometimes, when the second-grader struggles in school or when the adolescent rejects every expression of parental love, we rely on this imaginative ability to picture a better day.

Wisdom provides vision, hope, and a bit of foresight.

God of all wisdom, help me see large today, especially concerning [name]. Help me observe this person's personality and talents and, in faith, thank you for the better days you already see.

Sunday

Find your favorite chair or outdoor spot and stay there awhile, praying your gratitude for the gifts you have received.

God who loves my soul, please embrace me with calm and hope.

Ignatian Focus: The Two Standards

See a great plain, comprising the whole region about Jerusalem, where the sovereign Commander-in-Chief of all the good is Christ our Lord; and another plain about the region of Babylon, where the chief of the enemy is Lucifer.

—SE 138

Two different meanings of "standard" are at work in the prayer exercise called the Two Standards. When Ignatius wrote the exercise, he had in mind the flags used on a battlefield to designate and represent an army. He asks the person doing this exercise to imagine two plains ruled by two commanders: Christ and Lucifer. Each has a standard, or flag, around which troops gather. During battle, the soldier knows where his comrades are when he sees his army's standard. The question of this exercise is, which commander will you serve?

Today, the more common meaning of "standard" is something recognized as being the correct measurement of a particular quality. By what standards do I conduct myself? Against which standard of behavior do others evaluate me? We speak of having high standards or Christian standards. For the contemporary user of the Two Standards exercise, this meaning makes more sense; few of us today relate to battlefields with flags waving in the smoke.

We can ask the question: Do I choose to live by the standards set by Christ, or do I choose the standards of Christ's (and my) enemy? However we imagine our standard—a flag or a set of criteria—we must make a choice between two opposing ways of life.

It can help to list the qualities or activities that we associate with Jesus and with the kingdom of God. Yet, even "kingdom of God" has a strange ring in these times; few people who read this book will have experienced living in a kingdom as opposed to a republic, democracy, or other contemporary form of government. We might work with the phrase "Jesus' way of being in the world" or "this life as God intended it." At the very least, we can identify characteristics that we reject, such as greed, racism, abuse of power, and cruelty. The next task is to identify daily and subtle forms of those things.

Compassion: The Default Position

If you have chosen to follow Jesus of Nazareth, then you have already chosen compassion as your default position when others fail, trouble you, need your help, or behave badly.

This means that when a choice arises between compassion and something else, such as anger or impatience, there really is no choice. You have chosen a life path marked by the compassion of Christ.

Remind me, Holy Spirit, to walk the way of compassion today.

Courage: The Countercultural Way

If you have chosen to follow Jesus of Nazareth, then you are on a path that requires much courage, because the holy way is often countercultural.

On this path, on a somewhat regular basis, you will try to do what is difficult because it's the right thing to do. You will tell the truth, refuse to spread gossip, welcome the person who stands outside the circle, dare to stand up for morality, refuse to take revenge, and place money and power considerably low on your list of priorities.

Jesus, I choose courage to do what is difficult. Lead the way.

Creativity: Another Word for Faith

If you choose to follow Jesus of Nazareth, you will learn to live by faith more and more.

This means that you will discover creative ways to approach your life. You will learn to tell yourself, *There are always more options than the ones I see at first. There are opportunities and answers I do not see right now.*

> *God who creates me moment by moment, stimulate your creative spirit in me as I solve problems, make plans, and respond to my life as it happens to me today.*

Discernment: Saying Yes

If you choose to follow Jesus of Nazareth, you have by definition eliminated many decisions of daily life because saying yes to Jesus means saying no to whatever opposes God's way in the world.

Today, Holy Spirit, help me say yes to God's way and no to anything that opposes it.

Good Habits: Imitating Spiritual Teachers

If you choose to follow Jesus of Nazareth, you will imitate the habits of Jesus and those spiritual teachers he has given you, past and present.

What spiritual habit have you developed that helps you walk the Christian way?

Generosity: Free to Be Generous

If you choose to follow Jesus of Nazareth, you will become increasingly confident that God's abundance is available to you.

This means that you are free to be generous to others. You are not afraid of running out of any good thing because God is generous.

How can you demonstrate to others that you believe God is generous?

Sunday

A simple prayer for today:
I choose your way, God. Lead me in the week to come.

Jesus, you said that the Sabbath was made for humanity, not the other way around. May I use this day for the benefit of my soul.

Gratitude: The First Response

If you follow the way of Jesus, you will consistently look at what God is doing in you and in the world around you. Your first response will be gratitude. Your second response will be to join in God's activity.

Look around you this day. What is God doing? Have you offered thanks? How can you join God's activity in your small part of the world?

Lord, show me what you're doing today.

Humility: Jesus Is the Focus

If you choose to follow Jesus, your eyes will be on him and on God's kingdom on earth.

This means that your focus is not on yourself and instead is on divine presence and work in the world.

For five minutes this afternoon, sit quietly and refocus on Jesus. You might simply whisper his name repeatedly during that time. You might visualize God's love as a curative wind that brings healing all over the world. Focus on God the Father and Jesus the Son moving among the people you know, like a healing wind.

Integrity: Desire for Truth

If you follow Jesus of Nazareth, you will desire the truth more and more. You will desire to see clearly and speak plainly. You will avoid any words or actions that try to bend or change the truth.

Lord Jesus, I want to desire truth and always say what is true and to live with integrity.

Joy: Wonderful People

If you follow Jesus of Nazareth, then you will come to know others who follow him.

This means that a lot of wonderful people will bring joy to your life. People who truly care for you, people who pray, people who live by faith and hope, people who express love through word and deed.

It is true that some people say they follow Jesus, yet their lives tell another story. Now is not the time to concern yourself with those people. Take some time today to meditate on the true Christians you know and have known. Sit in the warm sun of that joy and companionship.

Openness: Wide-Open Future

If you follow Jesus of Nazareth, you acknowledge that you have no idea what is going to happen in your life—and you're all right with that. Who will enter your life? Where will you live? What work will you do? What challenges will you face? What impossible things will you set out to do? The future is wide open, but you go there in the power of God.

Today I say to you once again, Jesus, "I don't know where we're going or what might happen, but my only concern is that I'm with you."

Wisdom: Walking with Wisdom Personified

If you follow Jesus of Nazareth, you walk with Wisdom personified. You learn to listen, to pay attention, and to consider situations calmly.

For today, tell yourself this: *There's no reason to rush or worry. God gives me the time and information I need.*

Sunday

Find a place—in your home or somewhere else—that comforts you or helps you relax. Linger there as long as you can.

Holy Spirit, please help me quiet my anxieties and fears and rest in divine presence.

Compassion: Mercy Not Sacrifice

And as he sat at dinner in the house, many tax collectors and sinners
came and were sitting with him and his disciples. When the Pharisees
saw this, they said to his disciples, "Why does your teacher eat with
tax collectors and sinners?" But when he heard this, he said, "Those
who are well have no need of a physician, but those who are sick. Go
and learn what this means, 'I desire mercy, not sacrifice.' For I have
come to call not the righteous but sinners."
—Matthew 9:10–14

It's so tempting to get caught up in debates with others on theology, doctrine, even politics and public policy. But Jesus spoke plainly here, motivated by mercy. As we choose the way of Jesus, we will move more and more toward mercy and compassion in our dealings with others.

Notice today a time when you have the opportunity to choose mercy.

Courage: Choose Discomfort

Ask yourself a question that causes discomfort, such as:

- In what ways am I privileged, or not privileged, because of the color of my skin, my country of origin, or my faith?
- Which people do I tend to blame and vilify when I'm not happy with the current political or religious arena?
- Whose praise do I want, and how do I try to get that praise?

Holy Spirit, you know where my discomfort is, and you know which questions I try to avoid. Help me focus on the question that is most important today.

Creativity: Creating the Path

> *"I am about to do a new thing;*
> *now it springs forth, do you not perceive it?*
> *I will make a way in the wilderness*
> *and rivers in the desert."*
> —Isaiah 43:19

Divine love creates a path where none existed. This is why faith is so important; without it, we will fail to see the "new thing" God is doing, even if it's right in front of us.

Creator God, open my eyes to see whatever path you create for my steps this day.

Discernment: The Impact of One Choice

For your prayer and reflection today, make a list. Write down decisions that you've made—large and small—because of your fundamental decision to follow Christ. Some examples:

I chose to forgive someone.

I made different choices about how to spend my money.

I let go of my schedule that afternoon because someone needed my listening ear.

I participated in a small group at my church to learn how to study the Bible.

Help me, Holy Spirit, to see how my choice to walk with Jesus influences my thoughts, words, and behavior. I tend to forget some of the small but gradual ways my life has changed.

Good Habits: Beyond Self-Improvement

Every day, you become more of who you are. Every day, you reinforce some thoughts and activities more than other ones. You accept a habit of being critical toward a coworker, so you become even more critical. You allow yourself the distraction of social media or games because work is boring—and so you waste increasingly more time. You worry several times a day about how your clothes look, and it gets to where you can't pass a mirror or glass surface without checking (and judging) your appearance. These are little habits of formation.

Consider becoming more proactive about forming yourself. If you're going to have habits, at least make them better ones. Perhaps you can decide to praise another person in a specific way every day. You then begin looking for reasons to praise people more often. It becomes a habit; you are forming yourself to encourage and lift up others. Perhaps you choose to turn off social media and use your time more purposefully.

What small habit of formation would help you right now?

Dear God, I avoid "self-improvement" sometimes because so often it fails and leaves me even more discouraged. But I do want to create some small but important habits that will gradually form me into the person I desire to be. Give me the courage to start today.

••• **THE TWO STANDARDS / WEEK 19** •••

Generosity: Benefit of the Doubt

Every good Christian is more ready to put a good interpretation on
another's statement than to condemn it as false.
—SE 22

Ignatius was speaking to spiritual directors when he wrote these words. He was encouraging them to assume the best while they listened to their directees; they must not rush to the conclusion that this person was saying anything heretical or displeasing to God. Perhaps Ignatius—who had to defend himself more than once before the Inquisition—knew that humans are quick to judge and to take words the wrong way.

We all know that it can be hard to interpret things other people say in a good way, that we sometimes are more ready with a bad interpretation. For example, if a person says something to me that I don't quite understand, my tendency is to read a negative meaning into it. Then I become angry or offended because of my "bad" interpretation.

As you take part in multiple conversations today, try to apply this principle of "good interpretation."

Holy Spirit, nudge me when I veer into "bad interpretation"
territory.

Sunday

Sit down to a meal with someone you love—or with a whole room full of people you love.

Lord Jesus, help my whole self—body, mind, spirit—express true prayer today.

Gratitude: Two Kinds of People

As [Jesus] entered a village, ten lepers approached him. Keeping their distance, they called out, saying, "Jesus, Master, have mercy on us!" When he saw them, he said to them, "Go and show yourselves to the priests." And as they went, they were made clean. Then one of them, when he saw that he was healed, turned back, praising God with a loud voice. He prostrated himself at Jesus' feet and thanked him. And he was a Samaritan. Then Jesus asked, "Were not ten made clean? But the other nine, where are they? Was none of them found to return and give praise to God except this foreigner?" Then he said to him, "Get up and go on your way; your faith has made you well."

—Luke 17:12–19

This story is a sad commentary, isn't it? Only one out of ten people—all of whom received the same miraculous healing—thought to return to the healer to give thanks and praise.

What about our own typical prayers? Most of them are requests. Once a prayer is answered, do we pause and thank God? Or do we move on to the next request?

Review some of your prayers and make a point to thank God for those that have been answered.

Humility: Wait for God

Humble yourselves therefore under the mighty hand of God, so that he may exalt you in due time.

—1 Peter 5:6

God will exalt us when the time is right. A day will come when we're in the spotlight or have special influence. We may even receive praise or honor. Our responsibility, though, is to humble ourselves and do what is right. We follow God's way and receive what it brings to us.

God, I don't know what will happen today. Maybe I'll work hard and receive no credit at all. Maybe I'll be called upon to step up and take action that will bring more attention to me. Whatever the case, remind me that I stand for the values of your kingdom on earth.

Integrity: What You Say

Again, you have heard that it was said to those of ancient times, "You shall not swear falsely, but carry out the vows you have made to the Lord." But I say to you, Do not swear at all, either by heaven, for it is the throne of God, or by the earth, for it is his footstool, or by Jerusalem, for it is the city of the great King. And do not swear by your head, for you cannot make one hair white or black. Let your word be "Yes, Yes" or "No, No"; anything more than this comes from the evil one.
—Matthew 5:33–37

Let's relate Jesus' words to here and now:

- Don't pile up promises.
- Don't complicate your communication.
- Do what you say you'll do.
- Know when it's time to be quiet.

Sometime today, do a brave thing and review what you've said so far. Ask these simple, powerful questions:

- Did I tell the truth?
- Did I exaggerate or slant the telling for my own benefit?
- Did I commit to action I might not be able to carry out?
- Did I overexplain what should have been a simple answer?
- Did I keep talking when it would have been better to stop?

Lord, show me where my speech works against integrity.

Joy: Through the Gate to Abundant Life

I am the gate. Whoever enters by me will be saved, and will come in and go out and find pasture. The thief comes only to steal and kill and destroy. I came that they may have life, and have it abundantly.
—John 10:9–10

Jesus, comparing himself to a good shepherd, invites us into his sheepfold. There we will find abundant life. Perhaps we choose Christ because we see doing so as the "right" way. We want to do the right thing and be the right kind of people. What does Jesus want? Our joy. Our experience of an abundant, fulfilling life. Becoming better people is merely a by-product of dwelling in the love of God.

Jesus says to me, this very moment, "I want you to have abundant life."

What do I say in response?

Openness: "Here I am."

Then I heard the voice of the Lord saying, "Whom shall I send, and who will go for us?" And I said, "Here am I; send me!"
—Isaiah 6:8

Sometimes, God asks for a volunteer.

God does not force us to do anything but invites us to join divine work in the world. The Jesuit writer and spiritual director William A. Barry sometimes refers to this as God asking us to take part in the family business. That business is redemption of the world, healing of the world, our feet and hands and minds and words bringing God's love into the world.

That's rather mind-blowing, that God of the universe asks for our participation in whatever God is doing.

Dear God, develop my vision for what your kingdom on earth looks like. Show me how my gifts and desires fit into your actions in this world.

Wisdom: The Right Clues

*But the wisdom from above is first pure, then peaceable, gentle,
willing to yield, full of mercy and good fruits, without a trace of
partiality or hypocrisy.*
—James 3:17

What a helpful list of clues! If I want to know if my thoughts
are God-inspired, then I judge them accordingly. Will this idea or
plan encourage peace? Is it gentle and respectful, or coercive and
manipulative? Does it lead to mercy? Is it truthful?

Here's an experiment. Pick one of your favorite theories,
ideas, political opinions, or life strategies and assess it using the
standards of James 3:17.

How did that go?

*God, I am willing to change my thoughts if they do not
exemplify your ways.*

Sunday

A Scripture for meditation: 1 Corinthians 13.

*God of the universe, may I rest in the confidence that you
uphold me with the very breath of life.*

Ignatian Focus: Spiritual Freedom

Freedom is the ability to make wise choices in the midst of emotional turmoil.
Freedom is a stance toward life that opens you to possibility and cultivates a positive outlook.
Freedom removes interior constraints so that you can follow the best way.
Freedom means that you truly have a choice.
Freedom moves you to greater love.
Freedom brings peace and makes a way for contentment.
—Vinita Hampton Wright, *Praying Freedom*

Who doesn't want to be free? And don't we believe that Jesus wants us to be free—from sin and falsehood and suffering? He came to set us free.

Spiritual freedom in the Ignatian view is the ability to love and follow God because no other attachments, sins, or loyalties prevent us from doing so. This freedom involves the truth, because only through truthful evaluation can we learn how we are unfree. What loves and attachments get in the way of our openness to God's desires for us? What biases and fears prevent us from making the best choices? To what sins do we cling out of the misguided belief that they help or satisfy us?

We can suspect a lack of spiritual freedom when our thoughts, words, and actions are powered by fear, resistance, panic, an overblown sense of obligation, or any other form of feeling desperate or pushed into a corner. The Holy Spirit does not force or coerce us but invites us to participate in God's life and activity in this world. Sometimes we do sense urgency about a matter because a choice must be made sooner rather than later. Also, we can feel desperately in need of God's help or comfort. But these feelings and intuitions occur as we learn to trust God's love and guidance.

Freedom applies to sin, addiction, and poor mental or emotional health. It also applies to good works, pleasure, and relationships. Can we open our hands and hearts at any moment—to let go of what paralyzes us and to receive what God has for us?

Compassion: Distracted from Compassion

What prevents you from being compassionate today? Are you distracted by your own problems? Focused on getting your work done? Overwhelmed by too many news stories about too many people in need?

Try this: take a step back, away from what is dominating your attention.

Then say this simple prayer:

I am willing to become spiritually free enough to care about another person today. Please show me who that person is.

Courage: Trying the New Way

Becoming spiritually free makes it possible to act with courage. A spiritually free person can choose to say yes or no, to embark on a new activity or to cease an activity that has become counterproductive. A spiritually free person can consider multiple options rather than strive for a particular outcome.

Giving up your insistence on a certain outcome or plan of action will move you into a mental and emotional place that feels less certain or comfortable. And this is the place where courage develops—courage to try a new way, to consider another viewpoint or strategy.

Today, consider a new option for one activity. It could be as minor as having something different for breakfast, or as major as a change in your budget for the year. Make this choice with care and prayer, but allow yourself to edge into a place that requires a bit of courage.

Creativity: Not Coercion

Creativity cannot thrive in an environment of judgment, coercion, or fear. Just imagine what it would be like if another person were hindering your creativity:

- You try to paint or draw while someone is looking over your shoulder, making negative remarks.
- You are forced to sing a song because someone with authority wants to use your talent without respecting you.
- You try to plan a project for a boss who has just said to you, "If this doesn't succeed, it's all your fault."

If you do not have spiritual freedom, you can sabotage your own creativity without anyone else being involved:

- You try to write a story while your inner critic keeps up the negative chatter: *You can't write! What makes you think you have anything to say?*
- You agree to be part of an artistic endeavor not because you enjoy it but because you feel you have no choice. They really need volunteers, and you have the skill.
- You struggle to create something that is important to you—a work of art or a nice meal for friends—but you insist that it be perfect in every way. When it isn't, you lose energy and interest.

Reflect on an area in your life in which you feel—from others or yourself—criticized, coerced, or fearful, and talk to God about it.

Discernment: What Does God Desire?

In the Christian tradition, discernment is the process by which a person discovers what God desires. Or, to put it another way, a person makes the best choice—best for the person, best for other people, best for God's purposes in the world.

Because you and I cannot see the bigger picture or understand all the complexities of a situation, we need God's help to make good choices. We need to listen to the Spirit, to draw on our intellect and intuition and the counsel of others.

However, the process becomes skewed if, while trying to discern, we also try to force the outcome we want. Our desires are important and need to be included in discernment, but when we lean too hard for an outcome, it prevents us from receiving all the important information, such as the wise words of a mentor or God's still, small voice.

If you are moving toward a decision this day or week, ask for the grace to detect when you push too hard toward an outcome or when you deflect information God is sending your way.

Good Habits: Helpful Statements

Form a habit of spiritual freedom. Create a few simple statements to repeat to yourself or to include in your regular prayers. For instance:

"If I feel backed into a corner, that's not spiritual freedom."

"Lord, I am willing to want what you want—even if I don't yet want it!"

"What am I clinging to, and why?"

"Whose authority is influencing my decisions—and is that good or bad?"

Generosity: What Gets in the Way?

If you are not grasping after honor or status or power or possession, then you will be spiritually free to be generous to others.

What gets in the way of my generosity?

- Fear that there won't be enough (money, opportunity, credit) for me
- Concern that generosity will make me look weak
- Worry that helping others get ahead will diminish my own progress

Answer this question and make it the focus of your prayer today: In what area of my life is it most difficult for me to be generous?

Sunday

Do something today that you enjoy, something that helps you relax and have fun.

Heavenly Father, open my heart to Sabbath rest.

Gratitude: Hands Open

Gratitude leads to openness. A grateful person goes through life with hands open to receive God's gifts. It's difficult to be grateful with clenched fists. Not having spiritual freedom is a lot like walking around with clenched fists, fearful of letting go of something. A clenched fist stays defensive, ready to strike back. A clenched fist cannot receive a gift.

An open hand is a beautiful image of spiritual freedom, one that shows you have opened your life to divine possibilities. To continue your growth in freedom, stoke your gratitude, and name the gifts you already have.

In today's prayer, name some gifts for which you are thankful. And—this is important—while you pray, open your hands, palms toward the sky.

Humility: What Others Think

Can you imagine how liberating it would be if you could simply stop worrying about where you stand with other people? If you could stop—even for a single day—thinking about what others might be thinking about you? If you could cease to be concerned about your status at work or in the family or neighborhood? Go ahead: try to imagine what that would feel like.

When we are intentional about developing humility, which takes our focus off status and redirects it toward others—we enter a very free space indeed. The pressure is off to be better or special or noticed or honored. We can channel our personal power into kind and gentle work that benefits everyone.

Today, when you notice that you're worrying about yourself—again!—whisper, "Why should this be about me, anyway?"

Integrity: No Alternative Reality

I once commented to a group of friends, "I don't lie because I have such a bad memory!" We had a good laugh because we all knew that once you start playing with the truth, you create an alternative story that you must now remember. It takes work to maintain a lie, to keep the story straight, to stick with a disguise, to build a logical framework around falsehood.

If you're reading this book, you're probably not the sort of person who makes a practice of lying. But, if you're like most people, you do create your own alternative reality in subtle ways. For example, it's easier to work long hours than to go home and deal with the strained marriage or the angry teenager, so you tell yourself that all those extra hours are really for the good of the family. Because you panic every time you look at your finances, you tell yourself that every person you know is in debt and that this is normal and okay.

Free yourself from the burden of maintaining a lie, whether a big or a little one. The first step is a prayer something like this:

Holy Spirit, please alert me when I'm slipping into some false, alternative mind-set.

Joy: Enjoy One Thing

What gives you joy? Name anything and everything that gives you joy: activities, places, relationships, music, whatever fills you up with that deep and lasting happiness.

Make a point to enjoy one thing today that gives you joy. The experience of joy is a gift from God, and God would not give us gifts if we were not intended to savor them. An important aspect of spiritual freedom is that we are free to receive whatever God has designed for our joy and abundance.

God who showers my life with gifts, today, this is the joy I will savor . . .

Openness: The Opposite of Judgmental

I have noticed that creative people tend to have eclectic tastes, be it in food or in friends. When I visit with artist friends at a nearby gallery, I find myself in a diverse, interesting, and fun group. Creative types nurture their creativity by remaining open to whatever they might discover or experience.

I find also that such openness seems to eliminate judgmental attitudes. In being open toward you, I have no reason to judge the way you paint or dress. I'm not concerned about your taste in music or how tidy your house is. My openness also helps free you to be who you are.

There's probably someone in your life who needs some encouragement to be who she or he is without anxiety or self-judgment. Find a way to express an open heart to that person.

Wisdom: It's Bigger Than You

Something important to remember about wisdom: It's bigger than any one individual. A writer taps into wisdom and thus writes better than she can write. A spiritual director taps wisdom and listens better than he can listen. A parent taps wisdom and becomes a better mom than she is. Wisdom takes us beyond ourselves. True wisdom, which comes from God and is grounded in love, connects us to the wisdom of the saints and the ages. In this way, wisdom frees us from ourselves.

As we submit to wisdom, we allow ourselves to float out into the deep waters of divine-and-human existence. We are held up by the stories that came before us and by the people who walked this way before.

Ask for wisdom this day. Make up your mind to say yes when it extends the invitation.

Sunday

Give up an argument today—whether one you're tempted to have with someone now or an imaginary argument you'd like to have with someone. Give it up. Honor the Sabbath by letting go of anger and the need to be right.

Holy Spirit, please guide my thoughts and meditations this day.

Compassion: Bonds of Love

What does compassion have to do with spiritual freedom? Compassion ties us to other people with the bonds of love. But if we are bonded by love, how can we be free? Wouldn't it be more liberating not to care about anyone? Refusing to become compassionate will spare us the heartache of involvement—and we all know that being involved with other people brings heartache, too. Compassion, like any form of love, renders us vulnerable.

Love leads to complications, doesn't it? Love always costs us something.

And yet, we choose to love and to allow the fibers of our hearts to intertwine with those of other hearts. We choose to weep when others weep and laugh when they laugh. In our Christlike compassion, we determine to walk with people through illness or divorce or other devastating loss. In saying yes to Christlikeness, we abide in Jesus the Christ, who gives us what we need in order to love. And so we discover that love itself is the freedom. We are free to suffer heartache because we are intimately related to the One who can heal us.

What do you fear will be the cost, the entanglement, of compassion? Speak truthfully about this to Christ in prayer.

Courage: Held in Christ's Presence

But we have this treasure in clay jars, so that it may be made clear that this extraordinary power belongs to God and does not come from us. We are afflicted in every way, but not crushed; perplexed, but not driven to despair; persecuted, but not forsaken; struck down, but not destroyed; always carrying in the body the death of Jesus, so that the life of Jesus may also be made visible in our bodies.
—2 Corinthians 4:7–10

The apostle Paul had come to understand that everything he experienced was held in God's larger purpose and in Christ's continuing presence. Paul was therefore free to receive every moment in faith. This doesn't mean that he did so easily or never struggled when going through his many trials. He was free only in relinquishing his need to control the situation. He was free only as he trusted that Jesus' life was providing whatever he needed.

For Christians, courage grows out of trust. I trust that God's love will carry me where I need to go. I trust that Jesus' life in me becomes stronger and more vibrant through every circumstance of my life.

Can you relate to what Paul is saying? Can you see your life held within Jesus' life? Use these questions to begin your conversation with God.

Creativity: Jump Ahead Ten Years

When the details of a given day or week get to be frustrating or discouraging, ask yourself, *What do I want to be doing—who do I want to be—ten years from now?* Dare to write down the first thing that comes to mind, and then summon the courage to look at your life. Are your present activities leading you to be that person? If not, don't panic. Give yourself permission to be dissatisfied with what you're doing now. Go ahead and imagine quitting the current thing and looking for something else that would set you on the better path. Allow the ten-years-ahead vision to release you from today's anxiety.

If you look carefully at your present tasks and worries, you may find that few of them have any long-term value to you, but some you may value highly. If you don't succeed at this class or that project, how important is it? If you hope to be married to this same person ten years from now, what can you do today to keep the relationship healthy? If you believe you have gifts that aren't getting any exercise now, what can you begin to do—even in small increments—to make room for those gifts in your life?

Help me think bigger and more long term. Life goes by quickly, and I don't want to get bogged down in details that won't matter even a month from now. I offer you my anxiety in exchange for creative dreams for my life.

••• SPIRITUAL FREEDOM / WEEK 23 •••

Discernment: Need for Indifference

I must be indifferent, without any inordinate attachment, so that I am not more inclined or disposed to accept the object in question than to relinquish it, nor to give it up than to accept it. I should be like a balance at equilibrium, without leaning to either side, that I might be ready to follow whatever I perceive is more for the glory and praise of God our Lord and for the salvation of my soul.

—SE 179

When making a discernment, it's crucial that I come to a point of indifference. This means that I am emotionally free to go either way, as God leads me to the decision.

This is not easy, especially if I want to go one way more than the other. I pray for the ability to become indifferent. I can work toward indifference by compiling a list of pros and cons for each option, countering my emotions with logical assessment.

Do I trust God to love me through whatever direction I receive? It helps to repeat to myself statements such as these:

- Whether I choose this option or that one, God loves me and always seeks to guide me.
- Even if I make the wrong decision, God continues to draw me to the best path for my life.
- Whatever happens, nothing will prevent me from receiving God's grace.

Good Habits: Relinquish Preferences

We must make ourselves indifferent to all created things, as far as we are allowed free choice and are not under any prohibition. . . . [W]e should not prefer health to sickness, riches to poverty, honor to dishonor, a long life to a short life. The same holds for all other things.

—SE 23

It can be disheartening to read this passage of the *Spiritual Exercises*. Who doesn't prefer to be healthy and comfortable? This level of spiritual freedom seems impossible!

Yet, we have learned from experience that, when in a given situation, we receive the grace necessary to accept life as it is. We might even experience joy and gratitude in circumstances that, to an outsider, appear daunting and horrible.

Can I look ahead and, imagining a life of poverty and suffering, hope that this is my future? Probably not. Can I look at my present life and perceive God's hand in it? Can I receive today's hardship with faith, hope, and love? For now, I am enduring. And while enduring, I sense another thing happening: I am growing closer to Christ, who also endured. Perhaps this is the real point of spiritual freedom—of indifference. I am free to walk alongside Jesus in every type of situation.

Lord Jesus, help me remember that indifference will free me to accompany you and grow deeper into our friendship.

Generosity: Measure for Measure

*"Give, and it will be given to you. A good measure, pressed down,
shaken together, running over, will be put into your lap; for the
measure you give will be the measure you get back."*
—Luke 6:38

Jesus assures his followers that they do not give in a vacuum.
There is a natural flow here between God the source of all gifts
and we who are free to pass along to others all that we are given.

I remember a time when finances were very tight in our
household and I decided to give five dollars to someone—I don't
remember who, possibly someone downtown asking for help. Five
dollars wasn't much, but every bit counted, and I winced a little
when I made the donation.

The next day, I was cleaning out a box of miscellany and
found—you guessed it—a five-dollar bill. I just picked it up and
laughed at this reminder from God's good universe.

*Lord, I want to be free to give. Increase my faith in your
abundance and guide my giving today.*

Sunday

Say to yourself several times today—or spend five minutes using the phrase as a mantra—*I am free to live as God's beloved child.*

Lord Jesus, help me go to a quiet place and find rest with you.

Gratitude: I Have Learned to Be Content

*I have learned to be content with whatever I have. I know what it is
to have little, and I know what it is to have plenty. In any and all
circumstances I have learned the secret of being well-fed and of going
hungry, of having plenty and of being in need. I can do all things
through him who strengthens me.*
—Philippians 4:11–13

In "any and all circumstances," spiritual freedom allows us to be
grateful, even content. This ability goes much deeper than a stoic
determination not to complain or give up. Such contentment
rests upon the faith that says, "I can do all things through him
who strengthens me." We cannot simply decide to be content; we
obtain this quality through our life in Christ.

I don't believe any of us truly grasps this freedom until
we have gone through experiences in which we know firsthand
Christ's strength. But we have these words of the apostle to
encourage us and help prepare us for harder times.

*Lord Jesus, at times I've become rather spoiled because I have
not been in need. May I be free to enjoy those times without
clinging to them or feeling guilty about the gifts I've been given.
Likewise, may I face more meager times in faith, clinging not
to needs but to your strength.*

Humility: Identify One Thing

Humility makes it possible for me to receive who I am right now. I don't compare myself to anyone else or dwell on the person I'd rather be or the characteristic I'd rather have.

This kind of self-concept can be difficult to maintain. But for today, try this: Identify one thing about yourself—hair, eye color, laugh, ability to make an excellent omelet, loyalty to friends, creativity as a grandpa, and so on. Choose just *one* thing.

Embrace that quality. Thank God for it. Allow yourself to take pleasure in it. Throughout the day, remind yourself of this quality.

Creator God, thank you for this one thing about myself that I celebrate today. This is precisely who I am, and I'm grateful for it and will do my best to nurture it.

Integrity: Not Your Own Doing

For by grace you have been saved through faith, and this is not your own doing; it is the gift of God—not the result of works, so that no one may boast.
—Ephesians 2:8–9

Isn't it freeing to know that we are not responsible for saving our own souls? Sometimes we forget this fact and act as if we might get to heaven if we work hard enough. But Scripture is clear—from Genesis to Revelation—that God has taken the initiative to love us and bring us into the holy family, the Body of Christ.

This doesn't mean that we can be passive, without our own work to do. Our spiritual work is to pay attention to God's presence and action. Our work is to say yes to God's constant invitation to be part of that presence and action in the world.

If we are honest with ourselves, we will acknowledge that God gives us this gift and that we choose whether to receive it. And, sometimes, we receive gifts from God that we do not yet understand. But we say yes because we also have the freedom to trust divine love.

I'm so grateful, Lord, that you have reached out to me—that you do this every day. I want to respond yes, but sometimes I can't quite get there. Thank you for loving me in those times, too.

Joy: Free in the Light

This is the message we have heard from him and proclaim to you, that God is light and in him there is no darkness at all. If we say that we have fellowship with him while we are walking in darkness, we lie and do not do what is true; but if we walk in the light as he himself is in the light, we have fellowship with one another, and the blood of Jesus his Son cleanses us from all sin.

—1 John 1:5–7

What is more freeing than fellowship without sin?

What is more joyful than a life lived in the light of God?

This passage describes such a life in union with God. Fellowship with God rules out falsehood, darkness, sin. To become free of those entities, we remain in this fellowship, gathered into holy presence by the power of God's love.

Consider what dims your joy lately. Have you believed a lie—about yourself or others? Have you dwelled with darkness: cynicism, hatred, vengefulness, resentment? Have you avoided facing sin rather than confessed it to the God who loves you?

God of light, please gather me up in your arms and shine understanding upon my mind and heart.

Openness: No Opinion

"You're entitled to your opinion."

Yes, you are. But you're also free *not* to have an opinion.

In this age of instant information and the continuous flicker of social media posts on our computer screens, we feel the pressure—the obligation—to form an opinion on every topic in the universe. Whatever the Twitter comment or Facebook meme, we must decide whether we agree or disagree.

What if you decide that you don't have an opinion? That you are still gathering information? Or that you are not invested enough in a matter to even need an opinion about it? How would life change if you decided this week to give up the option of having opinions?

You would be free to stay out of the argument.

You would be free to listen to others.

You would be free to allow your inner, God-given wisdom time to meditate on an issue.

You would be free of having to take immediate action.

Maybe it seems impossible to give up opinions completely, even for a few days, but can you choose one topic on which you will remain silent? Feel free to just sit one out.

Wisdom: Beware a Lack of Listening

You become wise through listening: taking in new information, accepting advice, absorbing the lessons of others' experiences.

However, it's impossible to listen if you've already made up your mind—because you don't need more information, you know what you're doing, and you don't see how someone else's experience really compares to yours.

The inability to listen to others is a sign of spiritual unfreedom. If you find yourself deflecting what someone says to you, it's time to consider why.

Do you fear new information because you might have to change your mind?

Does it make you feel weak or incompetent when you need help or advice?

Do you become stressed when you cannot make a decision immediately?

I want to listen better; help me figure out why I don't want to listen now.

Sunday

Give yourself time to look through a scrapbook or
photo album and enjoy your memories.

*May I be gentle with myself today and with the loved ones who
are with me.*

Ignatian Focus: Consolation

I call consolation every increase of faith, hope, and love, and all interior joy that invites and attracts to what is heavenly and to the salvation of one's soul by filling it with peace and quiet in its Creator and Lord.

—SE 316

Consolation is a state of moving toward greater faith, hope, and love. Usually it is accompanied by feelings of peace and gratitude, and by being assured of God's presence.

Like any other gift, consolation is a form of grace; we cannot make it happen. Through our good habits of prayer, gratitude, reflection, and right action, we prepare the way for consolation. We choose to follow Jesus. We choose to listen for God's voice and instruction in daily life. Consolation confirms that we are hearing God and walking on the right path.

Consolation does not always mean happiness and ease, however, because doing God's will often pits us against popular opinion and the constantly shifting tide of cultural norms. Jesus suffered by walking the holy path; his disciples suffered, and his followers have suffered throughout history. This means we will suffer, too. But suffering in the company of Jesus becomes an experience of consolation because we are living in harmony with God's purposes for creation. Thus, we can be sad and exhausted, or feel attacked from multiple directions, all while thriving on a deeper peace and understanding of who we are and what we're doing.

Sometimes God sends consolation out of nowhere, for no apparent reason and seemingly unconnected to anything we have done. Saint Ignatius called this "consolation without a preceding cause. For it is the prerogative of the Creator alone to enter the soul, depart from it, and cause a motion in it which draws the whole person into love of His Divine Majesty" (SE 330). This consolation reveals itself in our sudden understanding, flood of joy, perception of the spiritual life, acute sense of God's presence, or increased assurance of God's love.

Times of consolation give us specific experiences and insights that we can remember and continue to learn from as we reflect on them over the years. They also provide encouragement and strong memories when we later enter periods of desolation, during which our spiritual senses become dulled.

Compassion: Feeling Loved by God

Spiritual consolation reinforces our sense of God's compassion toward us. That is, if I feel myself loved by God; even if my situation is difficult, I am experiencing consolation. During such times, we are drawn toward God and become more convinced of God's love. We might see our sin more clearly than ever before, yet we see also that God's mercy and compassion counter our sin, save us from our destructive tendencies, and remind us that we are God's beloved.

For your prayer today, spend several minutes repeating this statement: *God is compassionate toward me.*

Courage: Building Us Up

Times of consolation can build up our courage for times of desolation.

This is one reason it is helpful to keep a journal—a record of some kind—of your spiritual life. When you are in consolation—feeling the effects of faith and hope and love, moving toward God, loving God and others—pay attention to how that feels. What do you experience when in consolation? Write about it or keep a record of it in some other way to help you remember what it's like to have faith and feel hopeful, to believe that God is at work in your life.

When difficult times come and when desolation threatens to wipe out all memory of God's love, your memory work during consolation can give you courage. You can hold on to what you know has happened in your life. You can wait out the bad times because former consolation provides you courage now.

Choose one way to do memory work during consolation. How can you help yourself remember times when you experience faith, hope, and love?

Creativity: In Harmony with God's Action

When we are in consolation, we are moving in harmony with God's action in the world. And because God's action is by nature creative, we, too, can become creative during times of consolation. At such times we are likely to feel freer, because our sense of God's love and presence is more acute. A person who feels loved is free to grow and explore.

Take advantage of the added emotional and spiritual freedom that can occur during consolation. Spend time simply imagining what new work you might do. Sit with a blank sheet of paper and ask the Holy Spirit to enliven your thinking and planning.

God who creates me every moment, I commit myself to living freely and creatively in your love.

Discernment: Beware of Overreaching

You might feel more certain of your decision making when you are in a state of consolation. You experience a sort of confidence because you feel that you are aligning your life with God's purposes. You sense the closeness of Christ's presence, and you might feel especially sensitive to the Holy Spirit's movement.

However, discernment still requires that we discern! While in consolation, we can be tempted to overreach in our spiritual goals. A sense of joy and purpose can lead to enthusiasm, which can result in unrealistic plans and commitments. If you are making a decision during consolation, take the same precautions as you would at any other time.

For today, identify some ways you move through discernment: prayer, spiritual direction, research, and so on. Clarify for yourself what has helped you choose well in the past.

Good Habits: A State of Growth

We cannot guarantee consolation or do anything to make it happen. Sometimes God grants us consolation simply as a grace; it is unconnected to anything we have done. And sometimes a person goes for long periods without experiencing consolation—this is certainly true of many of the saints.

We make a mistake, though, when we assume that consolation is completely disconnected from our own actions. Consolation is a state of growing in faith, hope, and love, and a person can cultivate her spirit and prepare it to grow in these ways.

What do you do regularly that prepares your spirit to experience consolation? Do you have practices of gratitude? Reading the Scriptures? Exposing your mind and heart to sources of wisdom and goodness? Do you practice a form of confession to help you clear your conscience and thus become more open to the reality of God's love for you?

Holy Spirit, help me identify one spiritual practice today that can prepare me to grow close to you and allow me to make space for consolation.

Generosity: Avoid Self-Focus

One sign of spiritual growth is openness and generosity toward others.

In fact, people who are enthusiastically "spiritual" but become increasingly self-involved are likely deceiving themselves. That sounds harsh, but most of us have met people who were extremely focused on their spirituality, and yet their so-called spirituality was not at all attractive to us. Some of the most irritating people are those focused on their spiritual well-being but in a way that is primarily focused on them—what they believe and experience and how God is speaking to them. This doesn't mean they are bad people; in many cases they are simply spiritually immature.

It is more helpful to ask myself, *Am I loving other people today?* than it is to ask, *Am I growing spiritually?* Focusing on myself can lock me into a spiral that closes my heart to whatever God is trying to share with me.

Lord, help me pay attention to others, whether or not I am in consolation.

Sunday

Sometimes we find it hard to stay still, and we keep trying to force it. I will sit here and rest. I will, I will!
But what if sitting still feels more chaotic than moving?
Make time to move slowly in a relatively quiet place. Perhaps walk mindfully around a park in your neighborhood. Or, if you move with assistance such as a wheelchair, glide down a sidewalk or around an indoor gym. The point is to go slowly and just soak in that you're alive in the world God created.
Such slow movement is not for solving problems or making lists or even praying in a specific way. This time is for you to relax and absorb existence. That's all.

God my creator, grant restorative rest to my body and mind today.

Gratitude: Draw Closer to God

What about your life today stimulates gratitude?

Think of at least one thing to give thanks for. If it's a difficult day, you might have to think a little harder.

Gratitude, all by itself, is a form of consolation. In giving thanks, you acknowledge God's gifts. In giving thanks, you draw closer to God. In giving thanks, you nurture your faith, hope, and love.

God, I thank you for [blank], trusting that my thanksgiving forms yet another connection between you and me.

Humility: The Fundamental Need

It's good that we cannot manufacture spiritual consolation, that we experience it only through God's grace.

We can manufacture pleasure—through food, drink, drugs, and experiences that feed our drive for sex or adrenaline. But we cannot satisfy our own souls. When we realize this, we grow in humility and understand that our fundamental need is for relationship with God.

If you long for consolation today, pray something like this:

God, I know that I am created to be in relationship with you. I know that my deepest needs are met only by your presence. I wait to become more open to your presence and more capable of recognizing it.

Integrity: Who I Truly Am

Consolation and integrity go together. When I live in harmony with God's desires and actions in the world, I cannot help but live in harmony with who I truly am. The more I embrace that I am a child of God, made in God's image, and part of the Body of Christ, the more I act in concert with God.

Also, when I embrace my true identity, I have no reason to create a false one. Various spirituality teachers have referred to the false self—the identity we create to cover up aspects of our lives that are frightening or painful. I am ashamed of something in my past, so I try to become someone else. But when I am growing in faith, hope, and love, I can put away that false self. God's forgiveness and healing are here to embrace me as I am.

What aspect of your life are you tempted to cover up or avoid? Bring this to prayer:

Lord, this part of my life just makes me want to be someone else. I'm trying to bring it to you, but it's so hard! Please help me.

Joy: What Matters Most

Joy comes to us when we connect to what matters most. We see this on the news when a reporter interviews someone who has just lost her home in a tornado or other natural disaster. She is obviously shaken at the loss but then says, "We're still here. You can build a new house, but what's important is that my family is safe." And we hear joy in her voice when she says that. She's lost her home, but her joy is rooted in the lives of her loved ones—her real priority.

What matters most to you? Identify at least one priority, one source of your deepest joy. How can you give time and energy to that priority today or sometime this week?

When you attend to what matters most, to what gives you joy, you create a place for consolation.

Openness: Do You Want Consolation?

Are you willing to experience consolation?

This is not a trick question. God's love is always available to us. God's gifts are always waiting for us. But do we want to receive them?

- Do you feel too unworthy to experience God's consolation? Is guilt pulling you back from consolation?
- Are you afraid to commit to a growing relationship with God—because you don't know what it will require from you?
- Have you overloaded your life with tasks, worries, and responsibilities, so that you are unable to savor consolation if it comes to you?

God who loves me, show me if I am somehow unwilling to experience what you have for me. Help me talk with you about it.

Wisdom: Savor Your Experience of God

We often think of wisdom as something we learn or as information we gather. But true wisdom is wrapped up in experience.

I can learn all about God and the Christian life. But until I experience God's action in my life, and until I put my Christianity into practice, I have not developed wisdom.

Periods of consolation provide experiences of God I can savor and meditate on. As I grow in faith, love, and hope, I also grow in understanding how these work in my life and others'. This is wisdom.

Spend a few minutes recalling an event or conversation or prayer that touched you and helped you grow spiritually.

Sunday

Today, sit with an image that is meaningful to you.
It can be a photograph, an icon, an Internet image
of a classic painting, or your grandchild's drawing.
Simply dwell with the image and gather up
whatever emotions or thoughts it evokes.

*God who loves my soul, please embrace me with calm
and hope.*

Compassion: New Every Morning

The steadfast love of the LORD never ceases,
his mercies never come to an end;
they are new every morning;
great is your faithfulness.
—Lamentations 3:22–23

One glory of living on a planet that turns on its axis approximately every twenty-four hours is that, for most of the globe's inhabitants (apologies to those living in Greenland or other countries close to the North or South Pole), there is the sense of starting over every morning when the sun appears again. After darkness and sleep, we get another chance to live well. If today goes badly, then we'll sleep again and wake up again to the light of day and try again.

The writer of Lamentations tried to convey just how steadfast God's love is. Divine mercies are new every morning. We may try God's patience, but it is impossible for us to wear out God's love or deplete God's mercy.

Thank you, Lord God, for how steadfastly you love me. You will not run out of compassion, mercy, or faithfulness toward me. May my attitude and behavior reflect this marvelous truth.

Courage: Don't Be Troubled

"Do not let your hearts be troubled. Believe in God, believe also in me."
—John 14:1

Jesus said often to his followers, including the inner circle of twelve disciples, "Don't be afraid" or "Don't worry" or "Don't be troubled." We don't have to guess at his meaning but simply believe what he says.

Do I want consolation, a sense of growing love and faith and hope? If so, I can take to heart Jesus' exhortation to believe what he has said.

Dear Jesus, you said quite plainly that we should not let our hearts be troubled. Please strengthen my belief in you and in your words to those who follow you.

Creativity: A New Thing

So if anyone is in Christ, there is a new creation: everything old has passed away; see, everything has become new!
—2 Corinthians 5:17

We can take consolation in the truth of God's ongoing creation in our lives. Divine love will always be doing a new thing in us. In fact, God can create something wonderful in a place of desolation: rivers in the desert.

Thank you, God, for this constant activity of creation in me, fueled by your love and grace.

Discernment: Recognize Corrupted Consolation

The enemy works subtly, distracting us little by little and corrupting consolation. . . . For example, if I find myself irritable, exhausted, and overwhelmed while working on some noble project I used to love, I should pause to discern how I arrived at this miserable place. This is a difficult but graced awareness. I should be thankful that I caught myself before more harm was done.
—Kevin O'Brien, SJ, *The Ignatian Adventure*

Consolation is "corrupted" when what began as growth in faith, hope, and love somehow changes course. The enemy—that entity that works against God's purposes—will, if failing to plunge us into desolation outright, work to diminish our present consolation. This makes sense. When I work on a project in which I have invested much importance, I can become defensive or fearful when that project is threatened. What I love, for the sake of God's kingdom, can become a point of vulnerability for me.

When I notice that I've become anxious, angry, or sad while involved in a worthy endeavor, it's time to "pause to discern how I arrived at this miserable place."

Holy Spirit, show me the specifics of the gradual decline I have experienced lately.

Good Habits: Back to the Examen

I look back on my day and ask God, "Who wore your face for me today? At what moment did you come to me through the words or actions of another person?" I relish that moment. I give thanks and praise for the gift of that person in my life.
—Mark E. Thibodeaux, SJ, *Reimagining the Ignatian Examen*

Once again, I benefit from taking the focus away from myself and shifting it toward others.

Perhaps I have experienced little consolation today in what I have done or how I have acted. At best, my day has been a level "So what?"

But another person has demonstrated love, mercy, kindness, wisdom, or joy. I am privileged to have had this person somewhere in my day. Just because God's image is clouded in my own demeanor does not prevent divine love from shining out of another human face.

Lord, thank you for [name], who reminds me of your presence today, and every day.

Generosity: Give Someone Credit

Identify how another person has contributed value to a project or an experience you've been part of. It could be the way your spouse helped the toddler stay occupied while you were helping an older child with homework. It could be the drudgery a colleague spent hours on that will go unnoticed because it's not work that shows. It could be a mentor who guided you through a process, an IT worker who solved problems so that you could get your work done. Someone, today or yesterday or lately, has done something well. Make sure she or he knows you notice. And mention it to others, too.

Don't forget that God will use your generosity as a form of consolation for others.

Dear Jesus, I get caught up just trying to make sure I do well, and it's easy to miss what others do. Open my eyes and show me a person to whom I can give credit today.

Sunday

Make a point to greet people warmly today,
conveying to them that they are valuable.

*Jesus, you said that Sabbath was made for humanity, not the
other way around. May I use this day for the benefit of my soul.*

Gratitude: For Whom Are You Grateful?

First, I thank my God through Jesus Christ for all of you, because your faith is proclaimed throughout the world.
—Romans 1:8

The writer of the letter to the church in Rome expressed gratitude for how the people lived their faith and demonstrated to the world the good news of Jesus.

All over the world, people are expressing their faith in God. They serve those who are suffering: victims of disaster, oppression, or war. They tell the good news of God's mercy and forgiveness so that people can be free from their pasts, their sins, and their bondage. They help marginalized people get education, healthcare, clean water, and nutritious food. They express God's beauty and truth through arts, science, and works of all kinds. They facilitate reconciliation between enemies and provide energy and hope toward solving problems great and small.

For whom do you express gratitude today? Whose work and witness in the world give you reason to be grateful?

Humility: Tested as We Are

Since, then, we have a great high priest who has passed through the heavens, Jesus, the Son of God, let us hold fast to our confession. For we do not have a high priest who is unable to sympathize with our weaknesses, but we have one who in every respect has been tested as we are, yet without sin. Let us therefore approach the throne of grace with boldness, so that we may receive mercy and find grace to help in time of need.
—Hebrews 4:14–16

If Christians could but grasp the truth of this passage, how differently we would live! Because Jesus allowed himself to be "tested as we are," we can trust his understanding of what life is like for us. If we truly lived by this truth, our trust in Jesus would be strong and constant.

Because Jesus has fulfilled the role of ultimate priest for humanity, we can approach God—God of the universe, enthroned in the heavens—with boldness. And in God's presence we can receive the mercy and grace we need. If we truly lived by this truth, we would turn every need immediately into a conversation with the God who loves us.

This is a tremendous source of consolation for us: because of Christ's humility, we can be bold, confident that God hears us and responds.

Meditate on Hebrews 4:14–16. Ask God to help you take it in, believe it, live it.

Integrity: Hearts of True Human Beings

I will sprinkle clean water upon you, and you shall be clean from all your uncleannesses, and from all your idols I will cleanse you. A new heart I will give you, and a new spirit I will put within you; and I will remove from your body the heart of stone and give you a heart of flesh.
—Ezekiel 36:25–26

The grace of consolation is God's action in us that returns us to our true nature as persons made in the divine image. God cleans us up and helps us turn from our idols—anything we have allowed to displace our love for God and others.

And then God takes away our hearts of stone: hearts that stay rigid with fear or stubbornness or an obsession with power; hearts that are too hard and impenetrable to be moved by mercy or compassion or tenderness; hearts too willfully ignorant to embrace the truth of who we are. God replaces those stony hearts with the flesh-and-blood hearts of true human beings.

What kind of heart beats in you right now? Has it turned hard and lifeless? If it has, in a time of consolation, you can face that truth. In a time of consolation, you desire the beautiful human heart God gave you at birth. Present your heart to divine grace and wait for transformation.

Joy: Story of Salvation

You have your own story of salvation. It is the story of God's action in your life. It is the story of graced moments, healed hurts, forgiven sins, new beginnings, growth, and personal epiphanies.

Can you write down—or draw or sketch on a timeline—a part of your story? Perhaps put down the details of a certain period when you were discovering that you had an interior life—a spiritual life that was bursting into bloom. Or tell the story of when your life changed course for the better or when you discovered one of your gifts and chose to embrace it.

Openness: Growing Trust

In any relationship, we add to our understanding of the other person as time goes by and we accumulate experiences with that person. Again and again we experience the other person's love, care, and honesty. Thus, we become more open and trusting toward him or her.

Every time we experience God's care for us, we add a bit of detail to what we know of God. As years go by and these moments of consolation help form our personal history, our trust in God grows and becomes stronger. As our trust grows, we become more open to God's love and purposes for us.

God does not expect us to trust completely from the very beginning of the relationship. God sends us times of consolation, and we accumulate those experiences, and our trust and openness grow as a result. Trust, openness, love—all develop in this ongoing process of relationship.

Write down what you know of God based on your times of consolation, when you have had a stronger sense of God's presence and character.

Wisdom: When Consolation Isn't Consolation

The enemy of human nature knows our weaknesses and tries to use them to convince us that we're doing fine when we're not. Even without an enemy in the picture, we are quite adept at deceiving ourselves when we don't want to face an uncomfortable truth. I can distract myself and make myself feel good by watching my favorite movies, traveling, and indulging in food and drink. Through excitement, stimulation, and distraction, I can avoid looking more carefully at my life to see that I am not living in concert with what God is doing in the world.

What gives you comfort and helps you forget your troubles? Have you been turning to those activities a lot lately? Have you managed to skimp on times of quiet and prayerful reflection about your daily actions and attitudes? If so, you can apply some silence and prayer and reflection today—before this pattern of false consolation takes you any further.

Lord Jesus, you know that I want to follow you—at least, that is my desire most of the time. If I have become distracted lately and have been fooled into thinking I'm fine when I'm not, please forgive this lapse of attention to you and your constant, loving movement in my life. Help me see where I went off course and then make the necessary correction.

Sunday

Allow yourself some time today to remember when you experienced peace. Linger with that memory and explore it: What caused the peace you felt? How long did it last? How did you respond to that time of consolation?

Holy Spirit, please help me quiet my anxieties and fears and rest in divine presence.

Ignatian Focus: Desolation

*I call desolation . . . darkness of soul, turmoil of spirit, inclination to
what is low and earthly, restlessness rising from many disturbances
and temptations which lead to want of faith, want of hope,
want of love.*
—SE 317

Desolation is a state of the soul that pulls us away from God.
Of course, we don't really move "away" from God, because God
is present always. But we do shift in our direction of life, in the
focus of our thoughts, and in our general emotional condition. In
desolation our spiritual state is off-kilter, no longer aligned with
divine truth, and no longer sensible to divine love.

Ignatius goes on to say that the soul in desolation "is wholly
slothful, tepid, sad, and separated, as it were, from its Creator
and Lord." When in desolation, our vision is skewed, and our
judgment also. We veer toward negativity and seem not to be able
to correct our course.

The author, retreat leader, and spiritual director Margaret Silf
notes in *Inner Compass* that desolation

- turns us in on ourselves;
- drives us down the spiral ever deeper into our own negative
  feelings;
- cuts us off from community;
- makes us want to give up on the things that used to be
  important to us;

- takes over our whole consciousness and crowds out our distant vision;
- covers up all our landmarks; and
- drains us of energy.

Some of these characteristics are also true of clinical depression, but desolation in the Ignatian sense occurs in people with or without depression.

Ignatius referred to being affected by the spirit that came from the devil and by the spirit that came from God. For him, a person in desolation has come under the influence of the evil or false spirit. In Ignatius's time, nearly everyone—Christian or not—believed in evil spirits: demons whose goal was to cause destruction and suffering for humans. Today, Christian beliefs about evil fall on a wide spectrum. Some believe in demons much as Ignatius did in the 1500s, and others define evil in terms of oppressive social systems, trauma in persons and in communities, and individual mental or emotional illness.

However we define or explain evil, each of us is affected by periods of desolation. We can learn to recognize it and act against it. We may be vulnerable to this troubling spiritual state, but we need not think of ourselves as its passive victims.

Compassion: A Gift of Desolation

No one wants to go through a time of desolation. But even so, it comes to all of us. The question is not how to avoid desolation but how to respond to it—and how to learn what we might gain from it.

One gift of desolation is our ability after experiencing it to relate to others who are going through hard times. When you have felt the death of hope in your own life, you will more easily notice when someone else is going through similar pain. Thus, compassion can be one response to desolation. You remember what it's like to feel disconnected, without faith, deeply sorrowful, needing answers that won't come. When you encounter others who feel like this, you will know better than to try to come up with answers or say that things aren't as bad as they seem. You will understand, from your experience of desolation, that sometimes the best you can do is sit with another, cry with another, simply be there.

Remember a difficult time in your life. What would have helped? What did not help? What do you know now that you didn't before you went through that period? Make some notes. You will need them—for yourself, when another dark time comes, but also for others who, in their dark times, can benefit from your experience.

Courage: What Does Courage Look Like?

Desolation calls upon our courage—at a time when courage is a quality we do not feel. We are too exhausted to have courage, too aimless and hopeless to look for it in ourselves. During desolation, our sense of faith is weak, and our sense of fear increases.

What does courage look like at such a time? It does not look like confidence or optimism. It might look like stubbornness. For instance, you are going through desolation, but you are married with three children. For you, courage is taking care of your loved ones when you feel little reason to care for yourself. Courage is speaking hope to youngsters when you feel little hope in the moment.

Spiritual courage digs down to reach what you know to be true, even when there seems to be absolutely no evidence of that truth in your life right now. Something inside you holds on and just keeps going. Prayer seems impossible, and sleep brings no rest, but you continue going through your day as if life is worth the effort.

Meditate on these thoughts today: *Courage is not the same as confidence. Courage is not the same as optimism. Courage holds on when these qualities of life are missing.*

Creativity: It Takes Different Forms

It might seem that creativity is absent during a period of desolation, but creativity takes different forms at such a time. For example, when in desolation, I create a new definition of *normal*. "Normal" used to be having a good day and feeling at home in my growing faith. During desolation, "normal" is "God, please help me" uttered a few times on a day that feels useless.

I create a new definition of *accomplishment*. When life is flowing pleasantly and I have energy for a job and family and ministry, accomplishment is having done several things well today. During desolation, accomplishment is seeing one or two simple tasks through, or it's my ability to go to work, come home, and speak a word of love to someone in my family.

God's grace during desolation can help us see ourselves with more understanding and patience. That's spiritual creativity when we need it most.

God, prepare me to be creative in my expectations when I face desolation.

Discernment: When Not to Make Major Decisions

It's best not to do major discernment during desolation. This comes from St. Ignatius in the *Spiritual Exercises*; it's also the advice given by many counselors and psychologists. Don't make a major decision in the first year after your spouse has died. Don't make significant changes (beyond what is recommended by doctors and other helpers) while you're physically ill or suffering from depression.

Our judgment can suffer during desolation. And each of us has weak points in this area. Perhaps whenever I'm in desolation, I tend to focus on the job I don't like and decide that I need to quit and find something else. Yet the roots of my desolation go much deeper than my job. Another person will conclude that the answer is to end a relationship—the problem must be with his partner rather than in himself. And so he goes from one relationship to another, often in concurrence with his periods of desolation.

Do you know what your weak points are when you are in desolation? Pray about this; it will help you prepare to discern wisely when the time comes, whether in the course of normal daily cares or larger matters that arise.

Good Habits: Form Healthy Habits Now

One of the best ways to prepare for those inevitable periods of desolation is to form healthy habits now. Spiritual formation can give you a solid foundation for the days when everything feels out of balance.

Your spiritual habits need not require large amounts of time or brain space. Here are three:

- Pray a prayer of gratitude at least once a day. Look back at the day and thank God for one thing.
- Sit for five minutes a day in God's presence and allow God's loving gaze to rest upon you.
- Every day take a ten-minute walk, and during that time meditate on something or someone you love.

These are just suggestions. For now, choose a habit you can form right away, so that you will be better equipped to endure a time of desolation.

Generosity: A Natural Antidote

Focusing on the needs of others is a natural antidote to desolation. We know now that St. Mother Teresa of Calcutta suffered years of desolation but continued caring for the poor, sick, dying, and desperate. Her life expressed God's love to the world, regardless of how she felt. Hers is a dramatic example, but what if she had stopped loving others when she stopped feeling God's presence?

What are your gifts to the world? What do you do well? What gifts and abilities do other people value in you? How do you give to others? Claim these gifts and determine that you will continue expressing them, using them to help others, whether in desolation, consolation, or somewhere in between.

God, I acknowledge this gift you have placed in me. I want to use this gift even when I am in desolation. With your help, I commit to this.

Sunday

Lie down for a while today, in a quiet place, alone.
As you lie there, imagine God looking down at you.
God sees your emotional state, your spiritual
struggles, your physical fatigue. God sees your
desires and your fears. You don't have to think
anything or say anything. Simply allow divine love
to hover over your life.

Lord Jesus, help my whole self—body, mind, spirit—express
true prayer today.

Gratitude: It Helps to Say Thanks

Gratitude is not our first inclination during times of desolation. Even if we practice thanking God for one thing every day, when we're going through difficulty, our words sound hollow.

Still, it helps to say thanks. Here are some suggestions:

Thank you, Lord, that I am still emotionally alive enough to feel bad. Even painful emotions are evidence that I'm still here and that life matters to me—otherwise, I'd feel nothing.

Thank you, Lord, that at least I have ways of talking about what I'm going through. I have learned enough in my life with you to have words for what I feel, and I can identify such things as desolation.

Thank you, Lord, for trusting me with this experience, as difficult as it is. I continue to grow into spiritual adulthood, which means that I have the capacity to bear hardship and use it to my advantage eventually. You know my heart and that I am capable of dealing with this situation.

Humility: Reminded of Grace

Desolation is evidence of my humanity: my weakness, my need, my sin, my frailty. I can choose how to respond to a situation, but I cannot control what happens. I can't even control how the situation makes me feel.

When I sense the weakening of faith, hope, and love in my life, I am reminded of how much I depend on God's grace. It's never a bad thing to remember that my soul needs God.

God who loves me, I admit that I need you every moment of my life, whether I am in desolation or consolation. I will always need your grace. Thank you for offering it so generously.

Integrity: Urged toward Honesty

One advantage of desolation is that it urges us toward honesty. The only way to get through the experience is to pour out our heart to God. You might even say that our prayers become desperate. Desperation—great need, coupled with our own failure to fill that need—moves us to face the truth. We become more willing to ask probing questions, such as the following:

- Have my feelings of desolation caused me to quit praying—or did my lack of prayer contribute to the feelings of desolation? (This can go either way.)

- Is there an issue I need to bring to prayer but keep pushing away?

- Could sin be at the root of this desolation?

- Am I trying to handle everything alone rather than allowing others to help?

- Have other activities crowded out spiritual practices?

- Could this desolation be related to a physical illness?

- Have I piled too many "spiritual" activities on my schedule, causing burnout?

If you're going through a hard time, choose a question to help you get to the root of the trouble.

Joy: Love What You Love

God has given us so many gifts—and most of them are what I would call ordinary graces. That means that they are sources of joy that occur naturally or that we can access without a lot of effort.

Pay attention to what gives you joy. Call to mind what has given you joy throughout your life so far. What did you enjoy as a small child? As a teenager or young adult? Was it music? Sports? Exploring the woods or fields? Building things? Creating plays or other adventures that could involve your friends? Do you still participate in any version of these activities?

God loves to watch us love what we love. If you become blissfully lost to time while working in your flower garden, then that joy is one of God's gifts to you. If listening to Frédéric Chopin or Alison Krauss lifts your spirit, then go to them in times of sorrow or doubt or temptation. If a certain color soothes you, perhaps redo your living room or bedroom in that color so that you're around it more. *Pay attention to what gives you joy.*

These gifts of joy are meant to help us during times of desolation. Use them when you need them.

Openness: Breaking Open

It's quite possible that desolation will break you open. This is not necessarily a bad thing.

When life is going well, you might slip into the delusion that you're doing well on your own. You are a problem solver, self-sufficient, doing just fine!

But when the world goes dark because you've lost hope or you struggle to believe any part of what you used to believe—when you are vulnerable and in pain—you might finally ask for help. You might finally accept the help that's been offered repeatedly.

It's good for us to become acquainted with our weakness when trying to stand alone; otherwise we would not learn what true fellowship is. We would not let in the people God has placed in our lives to love us.

Have you been trying to get through your desolation on your own? Who can you turn to for help? Who has offered to help? Are you ready to receive it?

Wisdom: What Do You Already Know?

It seems that when we experience spiritual difficulty, we go looking for answers, for wisdom, so that we know what to do. We forget, though, that God has been developing wisdom within us up until that moment. It's quite likely that we already know what we need to know—if we can just pause and search our memories and our store of wisdom. The Holy Spirit helps us remember what we have already learned. The Holy Spirit reminds us how to apply the wisdom we already have.

Do you need wisdom this day? Try reviewing past experiences similar to today's. Pray for help in remembering the wisdom within you.

Holy Spirit, you have been lovingly operating in my life for a long time. I trust that you have prepared me for the present challenge. Please remind me of what I already know.

Sunday

On this day of rest, do not look at your to-do list.
Today, rather than do, simply be.

God of the universe, may I rest in the confidence that you
uphold me with the very breath of life.

Compassion: Far from Our Transgressions

For as the heavens are high above the earth,
so great is his steadfast love towards those who fear him;
as far as the east is from the west,
so far he removes our transgressions from us.
—Psalm 103:11–12

If you are in desolation today, you likely feel the closeness of your mistakes, your sins, your weaknesses, your fears, your guilt. The negatives of life seem to loom over us at these times. The mind keeps replaying all our bad stories. Not only that, but we suffer from guilt that we cannot trace to anything specific. We cannot shake the nebulous, yet constant, feeling of *wrongness*.

These two verses from Psalm 103 can be your mantra today. As far as God is concerned, your past wrongs are completely out of the picture now. And if you feel a general sense of guilt but receive no hint from the Holy Spirit about what that guilt is connected to, consider it false and let it go.

Dear God, I whisper, over and over, the words of this psalm.
Thank you for moving my transgressions completely out of
sight forever.

Courage: Not a Victim

I hereby command you: Be strong and courageous; do not be frightened or dismayed, for the LORD your God is with you wherever you go.
—Joshua 1:9

It seems rather odd to be *commanded* to be strong and courageous. Either I am or I'm not, right? But perhaps I am accepting the role of victim. The enemy of our souls wants each of us to feel like a victim all the time. If we are convinced that we have no power over how we feel or respond—if we "can't help it"—then all we can do is passively give in to whatever happens "to" us.

The Lord commands Joshua to be courageous because God "is with you wherever you go." The courage is related not to personal feelings or failings but to the character of the God who is with Joshua, the God whose strength undergirds Joshua's small but growing strength.

Picture it this way: a child learns to be courageous and jump off the diving board because Dad or Mom is already in the pool, positioned to help if anything goes wrong.

It's so hard, God, to be strong when I feel so weak, to be courageous when I am tempted to fear on so many fronts. I want to trust you and draw from your resources. Show me how.

Creativity: Illustrate It

Try to express your desolation through art. Write about it in a meditation or essay or poem. Compose music to convey its mood. Use colors to illustrate what it feels like. Mold its shape with clay.

Then, present your art to Jesus. For now, this is the only offering you have, and it is enough.

Discernment: True and False Spirits

The false spirit: the "inner pull" away from God's plan and away from faith, hope, and love. The false spirit is also referred to as "the evil spirit" or "the enemy of our human nature."
The true spirit: the "inner pull" toward God's plan and toward faith, hope, and love. It is also referred to as "the good spirit."
—Mark E. Thibodeaux, SJ, *God's Voice Within*

The simple way to discern which spirit is influencing you is to ask, Am I moving away from faith, hope, and love? Or am I moving toward them?

If you seem to be falling away from your normal practices of prayer, worship, spiritual reading, and spending time with others—if you sense a growing distance between the person you are now and the person who, not long ago, enjoyed spiritual practices—then you may well be in desolation.

Other factors contribute to desolation: fatigue, conflict in a relationship, or your own unwise choices. But seeing the whole of this experience as a shift toward love or away from it makes it possible to deal with desolation on more than an emotional or logical level. It becomes a spiritual matter, with spiritual responses that can help you shift back to where you want to be.

Help me discern, Holy Spirit, what is going on with me right now.

••• DESOLATION / WEEK 31 •••

Good Habits: Spiritual Companionship

Desolation tends to pull you away from relationships and into isolation. You might say that the "enemy of human nature" knows that you are weaker alone than you are with others.

Desolation is a good time to pull good friends closer. Those who share your faith can pray with you and offer confirmation and support when you identify that you're going through desolation. Those who love you can speak plainly when they see your perception becoming skewed and inaccurate. It can be quite encouraging to hear another person say, "You're in a spiritual battle right now—no wonder you feel so mixed up and negative."

Lord Jesus, whom should I talk to about what I'm going through?

Generosity: Jesus, Remember Me

Then he said, "Jesus, remember me when you come into your kingdom." He replied, "Truly I tell you, today you will be with me in Paradise."
—Luke 23:42–43

Jesus was nailed to a scaffolding, dying by crucifixion, when the criminal being crucified next to him asked if Jesus might remember him—I suppose he was referring to when they were both on the other side of death. The criminal asked for some mercy, and Jesus gave him mercy and comfort, promising that he would see paradise that very day.

We can safely say that this thief beside Jesus was in desolation—dying and afraid. We don't know if he made this request of Jesus out of desperation or if he experienced true faith and recognized Jesus for who he was. But the man turned to Jesus. And Jesus, dying himself, answered with generosity.

When going through desolation, we come up with all kinds of reasons *not* to turn to Jesus. We feel guilty—*surely we brought this on ourselves*, we think. Or we feel that Jesus doesn't really care. Or we assert that many other people suffer more than we do, so we should just be quiet. At these times, we need to remember the thief on the cross and how Jesus responded to him.

Forgive me, Lord, for not counting on your mercy.

Sunday

Check in with a friend today to see how she's doing
and to let her know how you're doing.

Heavenly Father, open my heart to Sabbath rest.

Gratitude: Song in the Night

Why are you cast down, O my soul,
and why are you disquieted within me?
Hope in God; for I shall again praise him,
my help and my God. . . .
By day the LORD commands his steadfast love,
and at night his song is with me,
a prayer to the God of my life.
—Psalm 42:5–6, 8

It is possible to sing when the world is dark, when your soul is cast down. Sing of happier times. Sing of past moments, when you could feel God's love.

When sleep does not come, and you lie there in the dark with your troubled soul, sing the song that's in your heart. Delve into the pain or the blankness or the turmoil, and craft the phrases that fit. Try to include a phrase about "Hope in God . . . my help."

Humility: Like Jesus

If then there is any encouragement in Christ, any consolation from love, any sharing in the Spirit, any compassion and sympathy, make my joy complete: be of the same mind, having the same love, being in full accord and of one mind. Do nothing from selfish ambition or conceit, but in humility regard others as better than yourselves. Let each of you look not to your own interests, but to the interests of others. Let the same mind be in you that was in Christ Jesus,

> *who, though he was in the form of God,*
> *did not regard equality with God*
> *as something to be exploited,*
> *but emptied himself,*
> *taking the form of a slave,*
> *being born in human likeness.*
> *And being found in human form,*
> *he humbled himself*
> *and became obedient to the point of death—*
> *even death on a cross.*
> —Philippians 2:1–8

If desolation dogs your steps, take encouragement from Christ's example. His humility led to suffering and death, which he endured for our sakes. Through humility—regarding others better than we regard ourselves—we turn suffering on its head. Our humility fuels unity and mutual care. Desolation can do no harm in such an environment.

Integrity: Keeping Secrets

Ignatius warns against the false spirit's trick of getting me to keep things secret from my mentors and companions. . . . If I find myself doing so, chances are, the false spirit is afoot. When I am in desolation, I cannot trust my own judgment; I will need the objectivity and sensibility of the wise and loving people around me. Otherwise, I will be lost in my own private fog. . . . I will convince myself that

- *He wouldn't understand.*
- *She'll overreact.*
- *We don't have time to talk about it now.*
- *It's not that important anyhow.*
- *It's too embarrassing to mention.*
- *I need to work this out before I tell her about it.*
- *It will resolve itself.*
- *He's too busy to be bothered with this.*
- *She's dealing with her own personal issues right now.*
- *I know what she'll say.*
- *He'll be hurt . . . angry . . . disappointed.*

—Mark E. Thibodeaux, SJ, *God's Voice Within*

Are you keeping secrets about how you're doing spiritually? Are you making excuses not to bring up an issue you're dealing with? If so, make a point to break desolation's code of silence.

Lord, help me be transparent and get the help I need.

••• **DESOLATION / WEEK 32** •••

Joy: Stability in Rejoicing

> *Though the fig tree does not blossom,*
> *and no fruit is on the vines;*
> *though the produce of the olive fails,*
> *and the fields yield no food;*
> *though the flock is cut off from the fold,*
> *and there is no herd in the stalls,*
> *yet I will rejoice in the LORD;*
> *I will exult in the God of my salvation.*
> *GOD, the Lord, is my strength;*
> *he makes my feet like the feet of a deer,*
> *and makes me tread upon the heights.*
> —Habakkuk 3:17–19

Use the words of the prophet Habakkuk as your meditation, to sustain you through a desolate time.

Openness: The Desolation of Others

Desolation—spiritual and otherwise—touches other people, too. Go out of your way to read about what is happening somewhere else in the world. Choose a specific place or situation that's been in the news. Or, look for situations that are not so thoroughly reported because the people affected have little voice or resource. Take a few moments to put yourself in the place of the people you read about. What are their needs? Their fears? Pray for them.

God of all those who struggle in this life, please bring to the people in this situation what they need to get through it. Remind me, Holy Spirit, of their lives being lived far from mine and of their needs and gifts that you love and value.

Wisdom: Remember Other Pilgrims

It's good to remember that someone has already lived a life that is quite similar to the one you're living. Someone before you was the mother of three children under the age of eight. Someone else succeeded at a task that seemed impossible at first. Someone else faced cancer or a financial reversal of fortune or divorce or the violent death of a loved one. Someone else failed at one or more careers before discovering her true gifts and callings.

You're not the only pilgrim on this path. Many have journeyed ahead of you. So, when toils and troubles become overwhelming, find a spot at the roadside, and sit for a while and remember those other pilgrims. Ask yourself, *What would she have done?* or *How did he handle this when it happened to him?*

I am surrounded by the stories of other people, Lord, but I need to pay better attention. Help me gain strength and hope from all those other pilgrims on the path, not only the ones traveling alongside me today but also those who have passed this way before.

Sunday

Do something today that is mundane and not terribly important, such as sweeping the patio, looking through recipes, or hand-washing the car. In times of desolation, it can help to keep moving a bit.

All I can say today, God, is "Help!"

Ignatian Focus: Imagination

When the contemplation or meditation is on something visible, for example, when we contemplate Christ our Lord, the representation will consist in seeing in imagination the material place where the object is that we wish to contemplate. I said the material place, for example the temple, or the mountain where Jesus or His Mother is, according to the subject matter of the contemplation.

—SE 47

Ignatius recognized the value of an active imagination. He encouraged its use in prayer, especially when the person was praying with a Gospel story. The exercise instructs the person to imagine everything about the scene: sights, sounds, smells, tastes, facial expressions, actions and words of people in the scene.

This kind of exercise allows the Gospel scene to become more real and vivid. However, Ignatius believed that the Holy Spirit worked through the imagination, so his purpose went beyond creating a mental or emotional experience. He believed that imaginative prayer is yet another way for a person to open a door to God. He also believed that God enters all kinds of doors in a person's life—because God's love is that insistent.

We sometimes fear the imagination in prayer, therapy, or other interior work because we cannot control it. We can direct an imaginative exercise, but at some point, the experience goes its own way. To imagine is to invite an open-ended story to take place within ourselves. This does require faith, doesn't it?

Some people relish the imagination and feel comfortable working with it in prayer. Others have not experienced much freedom in this area. In whatever way we relate to our imaginative life, we can trust the Holy Spirit to fill that space and linger there with us.

Compassion: What It's Like to Be Someone Else

Did you know that it takes imagination to have compassion? If you want to experience compassion toward another person, you must imagine what it's like to be that person.

I can feel sorry for someone without relating to her or understanding her. I see her in a bad situation and feel sorry about it. But compassion goes deeper; it allows me to put myself in that person's place so that I understand, at least a little bit, what she is going through. And that takes imagination.

Think of a person who might need your compassion—a relative or friend or neighbor or coworker. Sit with your image of this person for a few moments, close your eyes, and imagine what she is going through. If you were going through the same thing, how would you feel? What would life be like? What would you need? What would you desire?

Now, using this imaginative understanding, offer the prayer you feel would be most meaningful for this person.

Courage: A New Life Course

When Ignatius of Loyola was recovering from a massive battlefield injury, he spent months imagining what his life might become once he was well. He imagined becoming a knight and winning the hand of a noble lady. After lingering with those scenes for a while, he would shift to another possible future in which he would become a saint of the church. He read stories about Jesus and about many of the saints, and these stories fueled his imagination. Eventually, Ignatius chose to follow Jesus with the same intensity he had applied to his life as a soldier.

Ignatius's life filled with challenges after that decision, and his road to becoming a devout follower of Jesus offered many trials and dangers. But in a way, he had already practiced and prepared for those times by rereading the saints' stories and imagining his own life on that path.

Do you need some courage today? Are there stories of other people that might fuel your imagination? Can you pause and imagine yourself succeeding at the hard task ahead of you?

Creativity: Imagine Possibilities

A creative life is one in which a person is willing to imagine possibilities and then take concrete steps toward them. Imagination supplies the vision, but creativity puts that vision to the test.

Creativity is willing to try and fail, to identify problems and come up with solutions, all in service to the vision. Imagination is willing to allow visions to form before the rational mind has figured out what they are or how to engage with them.

If you feel that creativity is lagging in your life, inspire your imagination. Give it some time. Free it to be fantastic or silly or scary. Don't worry if your imagination gives you an idea or an image you don't know what to do with. Your creativity will take it from here.

Creator God, show me how to fuel my imagination. Should I pay more attention to my dreams? Would it help if I put on some stimulating music and allowed my mind and heart to wander? Please help me work with this aspect of my life.

Discernment: Pretend You've Made the Decision

St. Ignatius of Loyola trusted the Holy Spirit to work through his imagination. He trusted in this enough to make imagination part of the discernment process.

If you're not sure which way to go or which action to take, imagine doing one or another. Act as if you've already decided, and then notice how that feels. For instance, imagine that you have decided to marry this person. Pretend it's already happened. How do you react? What do you experience emotionally, physically, intellectually? How does your spirit react when you imagine that you have begun this new life together?

Perhaps you have a decision to make that's not quite so life changing. Do you go on this weekend trip with your friends, or do you stay home and work on something that's important to you? There's no clear right or wrong here—either choice is perfectly fine. But is one choice better for you? Pretend you've decided one way, and then notice how your emotions and thoughts and body react.

Holy Spirit, help me trust you to use my imagination in my discernment.

Good Habits: Feed Your Imagination

We tend to think of imagination as an unpredictable, uncontrollable facet of the human personality. But people who create for a living know that imagination can be enhanced by a healthy dose of formation, of intentional practices. As a writer, I may have no ideas when I sit down to work, yet I make appointments with myself to write, and I have learned that if I show up regularly, my imaginative gifts will often show up, too.

Also, I can choose what I feed my imagination—what kinds of books and films, music, locations, people, and situations I seek to fuel my inner life.

Choose one way to feed your imagination this week: a book you will read or a walk you will take in a place that helps you relax and tend to your mind and heart.

Jesus, I believe that my imagination is part of the divine design.
I neglect this part of myself sometimes and don't always know
how to nurture it. Help me learn how best to nourish this
tremendous gift.

Generosity: Daydream with a Focus

How could you use imagination to enhance your generosity? You want to be a generous person, and you do give of your time and money and talents. You wonder, though, if you are missing opportunities to act in a generous way.

Try some daydreaming with generosity as the focus. Identify a person or group of people who would benefit from generosity—a neighbor going through a rough time or a team of colleagues at your workplace who need a success.

Put yourself in the place of one of those people. What do you desire? What is hindering success? What would it look like for someone to demonstrate generosity toward you?

Stay with this daydream ten minutes if you can, enough time to allow the imagination to do what it does. Then choose how you will respond.

Sunday

Today, go to a place nearby in which you can relax.
Try to spend at least half an hour there.

Holy Spirit, please guide my thoughts and meditations this day.

Gratitude: What If?

The Examen prayer, developed by Ignatius of Loyola, helps a person review the day prayerfully. One step is to look for where God was present in the day and express gratitude for that. This sounds simple, but there are days when finding a bright spot requires determination.

If you're finding it difficult to identify something positive about your day, try the "What if?" exercise. Look at some mundane part of the day, such as entering your workplace, and imagine a different scenario:

"What if I hadn't gotten this job when I did?"

"What if we had no building, no computers, no infrastructure?"

"What if someone in this building needs an insight that only I can offer?"

Jesus, help me see my life a bit differently today.

Humility: What Others Give Us

We're tempted to be obsessed with ourselves, aren't we? We worry about how we come across to others or if we receive the credit or thanks we deserve. Our mood goes sour after a look in the mirror, which reminds us of our physical imperfections. We expend an inordinate amount of energy just getting what we want out of the day.

Self-obsession is the enemy of humility. One way to counteract it is to imagine what life would be like without certain people in it. That is, we look closely at what we receive from that colleague or family member. We pay attention to how we benefit because of the bus driver or the doctor's assistant or the guy in the maintenance department who always knows how to find what we need. What do all these people give us every day, directly or indirectly? We can work against self-obsession by focusing on what we receive from others.

Holy Spirit, thank you for [names] and what they give me simply by their presence.

Integrity: Golden-Rule Thinking

"Do unto others as you would have others do unto you." That's a version of what most people call the Golden Rule. Imaginative thinking, though, can help us take this concept deeper.

Sometimes I need to consider what the other person would truly want. Perhaps how I want to be treated is not really the way he wants to be treated. So, using the Golden Rule in its simplest form isn't helpful.

Consider the difference between introverts and extroverts. In many situations, they want and need different kinds of treatment. An exhausted extrovert seeks company, because that's how he refuels. An introvert refuels through getting time alone. In one case, you hang out with the person; in the other, you leave.

People in some cultures need for you to look them in the eye when you're talking to them. In other cultures, eye contact is considered rude, if not threatening.

As you think about supporting or helping a specific person today, consider what life is like from his or her viewpoint. Then, prayerfully make an approach to offer what is needed.

Joy: Images of What Truly Matters

Joy is a quality of being that does not depend on circumstances. Joy stays grounded in the truth of God's love toward humanity. Joy focuses on what truly matters. Joy remembers the history of divine activity in a life.

Joy cultivates in us the ability to see ourselves through the filter of God's grace and Christ's redemption. We see our failure and frailty. Our minds are full of discouraging images—of our unkindness or impatience, of our resentment and sin. But we choose to visualize ourselves as God's chosen, God's beloved, people on a continuum of freedom and holiness. Through faith, we train our minds and hearts to hold these images of ourselves as God's people—and that's how ongoing joy is possible.

God who loves me, please fill my mind with images of me as
your beloved child.

Openness: Fear of Vulnerability

As God's people, we want to maintain open hearts and minds so that wisdom and love can flow into us and then through us and outward to others. Fear works against openness, closing us—if we're open, we're also vulnerable. How can we battle the fear of vulnerability, of open doors, of lack of control and the uncertain future?

We can imagine all sorts of futures. What if I don't get this job? Well, a job I don't even know about yet will appear. What if we have to move away from our home and friends? We will make another place feel like home, and new friends will come into our lives.

If you're struggling with openness, mentally play with a few scenarios.

God of Abraham and Sarah, who left home to follow you without knowing what would happen, help me have some fun with this uncertainty. Help me play with the possibilities.

Wisdom: Where Do I Find Wisdom?

I want to be wise, Lord. I don't want to make horrible mistakes. I want to make good choices. I don't want to hurt people.

Where will the wisdom come from? Who will speak it? How can I hear it?

Am I expecting wisdom from some people but not others? Do I look for it in books but not recognize it at the breakfast table? Help me see with eyes that do not fear new sights. Help me think with a mind unafraid of new ideas. Help me imagine that every person I meet today has a wise man or woman hidden away inside.

Sunday

Review and meditate on the words to a favorite hymn or song used in worship.

Lord Jesus, help me go to a quiet place and find rest with you.

Compassion: Observe Someone with Kindness

Have you ever noticed how easy it is to become irritated by strangers? How often have you glared at someone who talked loudly or moved too slowly? Today, allow kindness to move you forward.

When you notice someone—perhaps because that person is doing something annoying—choose to observe with the goal of feeling compassion. Why is she cranky and complaining? Has something happened that worries or scares her? What might be the cause of this man's delay in getting his car around the corner? Is he confused or distracted by pain or a problem? Imagine what sometimes causes you to be cranky or slow or too loud or not attentive enough. Say a short prayer for the person you observe.

Jesus, you saw a person's need more than her behavior. Help me apply your compassion to the people I meet, especially those who make a bad impression.

Courage: Confidence in God's Care

Consider the lilies, how they grow: they neither toil nor spin; yet I tell you, even Solomon in all his glory was not clothed like one of these.
—Luke 12:27

Jesus asks people to open their eyes and see how God provides. He compares lilies to the greatest king in Israel's history. We imagine for a moment God putting delicate color and design on the flowers at our feet. Can we imagine God caring for us? Can we allow a simple flower to stimulate our imaginations and strengthen our faith?

In this same sermon, Jesus tells his listeners not to worry about what they will eat or wear. We are not to worry but to look ahead with confidence in God's care.

What are you worried about today? Can you transform that worry into a prayer?

Creativity: Write Your Story

Today, find a quiet place and take fifteen minutes to write the story of your life. That's right—just fifteen minutes to cover your whole life. Write quickly so you can't think much about it. You may be surprised at the choices you make when you have only a few minutes to summarize your life.

Now, read what you've written. What stands out? What things did you leave out? Are there any surprises? What makes you feel good about this story, or not so good?

If you have time, take another fifteen minutes to write your life story again but feature a different aspect. Maybe concentrate on a certain period of your life. Or write only about turning points, failures, accomplishments, friendships, losses, or employment. Each time you do this exercise, do it quickly.

Life is multilayered, and as you explore your history, several themes will emerge. You cannot undo hurtful events, but you can certainly rethink them in the context of your life themes. You can even decide that in the overall scheme of things, some events are not as important as you have allowed them to be up to now.

Holy Spirit, show me different aspects of my life. Free me enough to pick and choose the events I want to emphasize and write about. Show me the themes in my life.

• • • IMAGINATION / WEEK 35 • • •

Discernment: Imagine the Worst

Go ahead. Imagine the worst thing that could happen right now—the person who could die or the possession that could be lost or destroyed or the job that could end or the relationship that could change. Imagine this in full color and vivid detail.

Now, imagine yourself coping with that worst-case scenario. At first, "coping" may consist entirely of crying a lot and throwing things. So, imagine long days, and weeks if you must, of crying and being unable to do much. Then imagine what you would do after the tears and depression have subsided. See yourself moving forward a step and then another step. See yourself making another start entirely: finding a new job or meeting new people who accept you as you are. See yourself taking time out of your difficult life to go somewhere more peaceful. See yourself sleeping as much as you need to and having the energy required for what comes next.

You have been through some version of a worst-possible thing—or you've been close to someone who has. You know what might happen and how you will probably feel. You also know—already—the steps you will eventually take.

See, you are wise already, with multiple experiences stored away in your memory. Use your imagination to play through past, present, and future. It can help you tap what God has taught you so far.

••• IMAGINATION / WEEK 35 •••

Good Habits: What Fills You with Wonder?

At writers' retreats, I encourage the participants to make a habit of doing "what fills you with wonder." This is especially helpful for times when we feel that our creativity is at a low ebb—we just don't seem to have much material or inspiration.

The imagination needs regular stimulation and exercise. What fills you with wonder? Looking at beautiful paintings? Going to a movie or concert? Playing softball in the community league? Hiking in the forest preserve? When you feel stale and tired, look for wonder and seek to be inspired.

How can I possibly become so uninterested and uncreative in a world full of wonders? Lead me to the inspiration I need.

Generosity: Reach Out to the Child

Sometimes you need to pay attention to the small child who still resides in your soul.

Find an image or some record of yourself as a small child: pictures, items from grammar school, references to you from other people's letters or photo albums. Find an old toy or book.

What were your loves and fears during childhood? Bring to your imagination the spaces and events that left deep impressions on your young self. Immerse yourself in that little person you were back then. Look at her picture and pretend that you've never seen this child before. Try to see what she needs, what she fears, what she dreams about.

Now, write that child a letter—to give her courage and happiness and hope. Tell her precisely how beautiful and smart and interesting she is. Tell her that God is really excited to have her life unfold on planet Earth.

You know, God, that I've not been entirely accepting of that child; in fact, I've tried to leave her behind. But she is still in here, needing love and encouragement. Thank you for giving me a fresh look at this wonderful little person. Show me how to love her better.

Sunday

Get lost in an adventure—a book, a movie, or a
walk around town.

*May I be gentle with myself today and with the loved ones who
are with me.*

Gratitude: Relive Good Times

A good memory relived can be almost as good as the event itself. And sometimes your experience in the years since can lend more meaning to the event when you look back at it.

Unlock your inner closets and drawers and boxes and take out those good times. The emotions from those times will return as well, like sudden whiffs of perfume from an old scarf in the attic. Allow those emotions to stimulate your imagination and help bring up the details of this memory so that you can relive it.

Lord, I tend to forget all those gifts I have—the treasures I keep confined to something I call the past. They are still your gifts to me. They can't be taken away. Even if my own memory fails, whatever trinkets remain, whatever remembrances others carry, keep the good times alive. Thank you, again, for the gift of today's memories. May I exercise often this ability to remember and give thanks.

Humility: Seeing Others as Saints

[Jesus] sat down opposite the treasury, and watched the crowd putting money into the treasury. Many rich people put in large sums. A poor widow came and put in two small copper coins, which are worth a penny. Then he called his disciples and said to them, "Truly I tell you, this poor widow has put in more than all those who are contributing to the treasury. For all of them have contributed out of their abundance; but she out of her poverty has put in everything she had, all she had to live on."
—Mark 12:41–44

Jesus saw a poor woman quite differently from how others saw her, especially the wealthy people around her. He pointed out that she, unlike the rich donors, gave everything she had. He saw her world, her poverty, her two small coins. But he did not compare her to anyone else; she stood on her own virtue, in her own category. And, in Jesus' view, she was in a better situation than the wealthy people who gave because they had disposable income.

Jesus, give me the spiritual imagination to see beyond what is obvious about people and perceive who they truly are.

Integrity: How Could You Have Acted Differently?

Sometimes I have to admit that I have not acted with complete integrity. I've told a half-truth or allowed, by my silence, for someone to infer an untruth. I have claimed to know more about a topic than I do. I have pretended to care about an issue. I've made a commitment that I knew I could not keep.

The imagination makes it possible for me to rehearse the kind of situation that tempts me away from integrity.

First, I identify a specific interaction in which I was not completely honest. Then I rerun the memory slowly and try to determine where my integrity began slipping.

Now I imagine how I would act differently if that situation happened again. I imagine in detail what I would say and how I would say it. When would I notice that I am tempted to be dishonest? What would I say to myself? What action would I take to remain honest?

Joy: Imagine a Wonderful Outcome

We are so proficient at imagining everything that could go wrong. Recently, my husband and I learned that a family member had suffered a medical trauma. The doctors projected a 50 percent chance of recovery. As the news sank in, the atmosphere in the room became dark and fearful.

Then one of us said, "This is not the time to allow our imaginations to jump to the worst conclusion." We knew that both of us were already thinking about a funeral and the impossible grief to come.

There is power in imagination, in the way we choose to see ourselves, our problems, our relationships, and our future. We can envision growth, love, success, and healthy recoveries. Or we can envision despair, worsening conflict, failure, and suffering. In prayer, we use imagination toward good outcomes. We envision God's care and help. When I stopped imagining the death of our loved one, I was able to pray, not out of fear and dread but from a place of faith-filled vision.

The loved one did recover. I'm not saying that our shift in imagination caused her healing—but it certainly may have helped. I know it helped us as we prayed.

Holy Spirit, enliven my imagination to create visions of your love in action.

Openness: The Benefit of Daydreaming

The imagination is a spiritual function. In the life of faith, it can cultivate receptivity to whatever may happen or whomever we may become. Daydreams are little exercises of the imagination. They are pressure valves that allow you to feel good about your life or to laugh at yourself even when you're in the middle of an uninspiring kind of day. Sometimes all you need to get through the present hour is to imagine the end of the day and a warm bed. Other situations require a more specific vision, such as what this project will look like when you've finally completed it.

Give yourself permission to daydream about yourself as more faith-filled, more willing to follow Jesus wherever he goes, more courageous and generous.

Give in to your mind's tendency to escape. It wants to escape for a reason. You're piling up too much pressure somewhere. Some part of you desires to become freer.

God who creates me at every moment, I don't know why I'm so afraid of my imagination sometimes. It's part of my life that you've designed to help me. So, I'll give myself permission to daydream. Show me how to use this gift. I want to be open to your possibilities for me.

Wisdom: Experience Jesus

They came to Jericho. As he and his disciples and a large crowd were leaving Jericho, Bartimaeus son of Timaeus, a blind beggar, was sitting by the roadside. When he heard that it was Jesus of Nazareth, he began to shout out and say, "Jesus, Son of David, have mercy on me!" Many sternly ordered him to be quiet, but he cried out even more loudly, "Son of David, have mercy on me!" Jesus stood still and said, "Call him here." And they called the blind man, saying to him, "Take heart; get up, he is calling you." So throwing off his cloak, he sprang up and came to Jesus. Then Jesus said to him, "What do you want me to do for you?" The blind man said to him, "My teacher, let me see again." Jesus said to him, "Go; your faith has made you well." Immediately he regained his sight and followed him on the way.
—Mark 10:46–52

Place yourself in this story—as Bartimaeus, one of the disciples, or an onlooker. Imagine the large crowd, the blind beggar at the roadside, the sounds and smells of the scene.

Listen to the exchange between Bartimaeus and Jesus. Notice the expressions on their faces, how they react to each other. Notice especially how Jesus looks at Bartimaeus and the tone of Jesus' voice when he speaks to him.

What insights are prompted in you as you watch this scene unfold?

Sunday

Don't forget to disengage from the stresses and issues of your workplace. This is the Sabbath.

God my creator, grant restorative rest to my body and mind today.

Ignatian Focus: Emotions

There was this difference, however. When he thought of worldly
matters, he found much delight; but after growing weary and
dismissing them, he found that he was dry and unhappy. But when he
thought of going barefoot to Jerusalem and eating nothing but herbs
and of imitating the saints in all the austerities they practiced, he not
only found consolation in these thoughts, but even after they had left
him he remained happy and joyful. . . . From experience he knew that
some thoughts left him sad while others made him happy, and little by
little he came to perceive the different spirits that were moving him;
one coming from the devil, the other coming from God.
—Ignatius of Loyola, *A Pilgrim's Journey: The Autobiography of*
Ignatius of Loyola

Ignatius did not pay much attention to his shifting emotions until he began to recognize a pattern. Happiness consistently accompanied his thoughts of imitating the saints; unhappiness consistently followed his thoughts of "worldly" matters—the courtly life with all its military and romantic adventures. He eventually concluded that emotions have a spiritual source.

Later, while spending months in prayer and writing out what would become his *Spiritual Exercises*, Ignatius maintained his respect for human emotions and the clues they offer. He did not give spiritual importance to every feeling a person experiences, but he believed that in the context of prayer and openness to God, emotions can work in concert with the Holy Spirit to help us understand ourselves and thus help us become more attentive to our interior spiritual movements.

Today, centuries later, spiritual directors continue to stress that emotions are gifts, indicators, and valuable components of the human personality. Every emotion is valid; no longer do we consider some emotions evil and others holy. It might be tempting to want to ban feelings of anger, fear, or anxiety from our life, but many of us have learned from experience that denying an emotion only drives it into us more deeply.

Emotions are especially helpful when we use them in prayer. That is, like the psalmist, we express to God exactly what we feel and why. The power of our feelings fuels our desire to cry out to God—for help, comfort, answer, or vindication. When we identify an emotion and face it directly, it can jump-start our conversation with God. In the moment we feel an emotion, much of our energy is located in it, so that's where our prayer can begin.

Compassion: Trying to Be Strong

Sometimes, the desire to be strong prevents us from acting with compassion. To many of us, being strong means that we don't allow emotions to sway us. I'm hurting but tuck away the hurt so I can get through the day. I'm joyful but don't want to draw attention to myself or look foolish.

Yet compassion requires emotional connection. If I act toward you with compassion, then that is possible only because I have allowed myself to feel something of what you feel right now. I allow myself to remember what it was like to get fired or have a child with a serious illness. Or, if I haven't gone through the experience you face, I try to imagine what it must feel like. Only then am I equipped to practice compassion, which is a form of being present with someone at a deep, heartfelt level.

Holy Spirit, today connect me to emotions that will help me
reach out to one other person.

Courage: Own That Emotion

Each day can be a roller-coaster ride through emotions. Joy with the lovey cat while you have the first cup of coffee; frustration on the commute to work; dismay at a coworker's curt e-mail; hope for the answer to a prayer; despair at yet one more delay in a process; anger at the afternoon news; sadness when you remember that your deceased mother's birthday is coming up.

Take courage this day and face every shift in feeling. Own each emotion as an honest response to real life. Permit the feeling to say what it needs to say to you. Then, speak these reminders to yourself:

- Emotions are not good or bad; they are clues.
- Emotions can provide information but need not tell me what to do.

Creativity: Draw a Picture

Here's an experiment to try when an emotion feels overwhelming.

Draw a picture of it. Use an ink pen or lead pencil or colored markers and fill a blank page. Notice which colors you're attracted to. Notice whether this feeling produces images—even stick figures—or simply swirls or scratches of color. Don't judge or try too hard. Just let it happen.

Then sit with it, study what you've created, and give this page a name, such as "Midafternoon worries" or "I still miss my dog."

Jesus, you know the details of what I feel and why. Help me with this, please.

Discernment: Emotions Are Clues

When you realize that emotions are clues, you acquire an important new tool for making good decisions. As you consider taking one action, pay attention to how that makes you feel: Tense? Satisfied? Hopeful? Confused? Consider taking a different, alternative action, and give the same close attention to how your emotional self responds.

Of course, emotions alone are not sufficient for good discernment; most of us have experienced the fallout of deciding something in the heat of emotion only to learn that we were misled. However, our feelings help us measure how ready we are to make a change. They can also warn us when we are about to do something that, in our deepest self, we know is not the best choice.

Holy Spirit, hover over this emotional mess that is me today.

Good Habits: Emotional Routines

What are your emotional habits or routines? You do have them—in fact, you probably learned some of them in your family of origin. Some families do loud arguments; other families hone the silent treatment to a fine point. Some families use anger to control others; other families use tears and sadness to gain allies.

As a grown-up, one of your tasks is self-management—that is, you choose to learn new emotional habits because they are healthy and helpful. What new habit can you nurture, starting now? Some suggestions:

- I will speak truthfully about what I think or feel but will do so calmly rather than to hurt someone or win a point in an argument.

- When I am sad, I will take the time to identify the source, and I will pray about it. I might even tell a friend about it.

- When someone makes me angry, rather than lash back or shut down around that person, I will write out precisely what has happened and how it makes me feel. I will carefully plan my response.

Choose an emotional habit you want to cultivate.

Generosity: Make a Safe Place

Today, show generosity to others by making a safe place for their emotions.

In a safe place . . .

- I am not judged.
- I can let my true emotions show.
- I can trust that my words will be held in confidence.
- I can receive words of acceptance, empathy, and encouragement.

What would it take for your office or your car or your living room to become such a safe place?

Lord Jesus, people learned that you were a safe place for their pains and fears and questions. Show me how to become a safe place for others.

Sunday

Imagine yourself tucked up in the safe place that is God's embrace.

God who loves my soul, please embrace me with calm and hope.

Gratitude: Notice One Thing

If you notice, every day, something that gives you an emotional lift—a good gift of some kind—then you will become grateful.

If you become grateful, you will develop the desire to express that gratitude.

If you desire to express gratitude, you may just end up praying.

Notice one gift this day. Just one.

Humility: Someone Else's Need

Here's a little project for the day, designed to help you grow in humility.

Whatever emotion you're feeling, look for another person who looks as if he or she feels the same way. For instance, I am often tired on my morning train commute. It's not difficult for me to spot others on the train who are tired, too. I see them and think, *I wonder what kind of job he has. Does he also work a second job? Does he have kids at home? Are there worries keeping him awake at night?*

It only takes a moment to stop focusing on my own fatigue and to silently pray for that other person.

God of all humanity, open my eyes to someone else's need today.

Integrity: Honesty with God

This has been a hard lesson to learn, but if someone thinks I'm angry, I probably am. True, it's possible another person misinterprets something I say or an expression on my face—I have been misunderstood as much as the next person. But integrity demands that I listen even when others misinterpret me. Chances are, the emotion they are picking up on is present, but a few levels down. Perhaps I cover it well most of the time, but it manages to bubble up periodically. My anger may have nothing to do with the person who picks up on it.

This is why our honesty before God is so crucial. Everything hidden will eventually come to light. Psychologists have long recognized that emotions we do not face will manifest anyway, often subconsciously, which makes it even more difficult for us to address them.

God, help me be honest about my feelings today. I don't want them to burrow in and cause trouble later.

Joy: Childhood Joy

What did you enjoy when you were a child? Spend time remembering this—maybe take a fifteen-minute break this afternoon to recall what you loved doing when you were little and had no responsibilities. What did you love before adults started telling you what you *should* love?

Are you involved, in any way, with this joy today? If not, why not? Could you make some room for this deep-down joy? Could you plan to participate with it soon?

Jesus, accompany me as I reengage with a joy from my childhood.

Openness: Our Labels for Emotions

First, tell yourself this: No emotion is right or wrong. Emotion simply is.

Second, ask yourself: Which emotions have I labeled off-limits, and why? Chances are, you have been conditioned to categorize emotions.

Third, pray:

> *God, you created me with a range of emotions, for good reason.*
> *I want to become more open to those emotions I have tried to*
> *keep out of my life because I was taught they were wrong or*
> *because I was afraid to feel them. Guide me through*
> *this, please.*

Wisdom: What Do Emotions Tell Us?

We are wise to recognize how we truly feel. We are wise to identify our feelings, sit with them, and listen to what they tell us.

We are also wise to balance our feelings with other resources, such as history, reason, and belief. For example:

- I feel that a person is trying to insult me. Has she done this in the past—do we have a history that supports my feelings right now?

- I feel ashamed to still be grieving after all this time. Yet any grief counselor or spiritual director will tell me that grief chooses its own schedule, and all I can do is be present and acknowledge it and work with it.

- I feel that my relative should be banned from the family for causing so much hurt through his addiction and law breaking. As a Christian, though, I believe in forgiveness and in Jesus' redemption of anyone and everyone. Perhaps the family should maintain some boundaries with this relative, for the protection of other family members. But vindictive and punitive banishment is not an option.

Holy Spirit, what resources can I bring to my primary emotion today?

Sunday

Allow yourself to feel your emotions deeply, if only
for a little while during the day.

Jesus, you said that Sabbath was made for humanity, not the
other way around. May I use this day for the benefit of my soul.

Compassion: The Lord's Suffering

[I] ask for what I desire. Here it will be to ask for sorrow, compassion, and shame because the Lord is going to His suffering for my sins.
—SE 193

Can we walk alongside Jesus of Nazareth as he faces the soldiers, the angry crowd, the torture of the crucifixion? Do we dare get close enough to feel some of what he experiences? The Spiritual Exercises instruct us to accompany Christ through the Passion and feel the emotional reality of his suffering for us. Without that emotional connection, it's too easy to simply rehearse the well-known story of the crucifixion rather than allow it to become personal. Use your emotional capacities to walk with the suffering Christ, who

- spoke truth to power, standing up for the poor, the weak, and the outcast, until those with earthly power silenced him;

- entered human experience, with its grit and struggle and proximity to evil, so that he could speak God the Father's love to us directly; and

- extended to us compassion, even when we ignored his message and persisted in our sin.

Help me connect emotionally to the truth of who you are, Lord Jesus, and what you have done in your compassion toward me.

Courage: A Good or Bad Report?

I influence others by the way I report a circumstance. I look at it with faith and courage and so present it that way. Or, I look at it with fear and pessimism and present it that way.

My report will stir the emotions of my listeners, and this can cause a shift in how an entire group of people perceives the circumstance.

I must cultivate faith and hope in the way I relate to others, even when we are facing difficult events. My courage can stir the hope of others. My cynicism can push others toward despair.

It's not a matter of telling the truth. The facts remain the same, but my outlook affects the way I present the facts. I want always to be pointing others to God's overarching love and watchfulness.

I call to mind now a time when I was encouraged—or disheartened—by the way someone represented a situation. How could they have inspired a different response in me and others?

Creativity: Get Lost in What You Love

There's such a thing as creative flow—the state we all enter when we are so engaged in an activity that we lose sense of time and place. Writers experience it; so do physicists. In the process of creative work, they get lost, in a good way.

I believe there's such a thing as emotional flow, too. It's a state we enter when we are doing something we love—it feeds the soul, develops a gift, or contributes good work to the world.

What activity stimulates your love, contentment, enjoyment, peace? Singing in the choir? Sharing a meal with your friends? Lending a hand at the food pantry?

Sometime this week, get lost in what you love.

Discernment: Death and Perspective

[I] consider what procedure and norm of action I would wish to have followed in making the present choice if I were at the moment of death. I will guide myself by this and make my decision entirely in conformity with it.
—SE 186

Ignatius suggests that if a person has trouble discerning which action to take, he or she can ask, "If I were on my deathbed, looking back on this decision, which choice would I want to have made?"

Death puts everything else in perspective. And for the person who uses the deathbed scene to assess a potential decision, the emotional reaction will be quite telling. When facing death, a person longs to have done what was most important. Time well spent brings contentment, but time given to lesser goals elicits immediate pangs of regret.

The deathbed imaginative exercise creates a useful opportunity for honest emotion.

Help me, Lord, to remind myself regularly that I will die someday—or maybe even today. May the brevity of my life here on earth bring out my deepest sense of what matters.

Good Habits: Complain Regularly

Evening and morning and at noon
I utter my complaint and moan,
and he will hear my voice.
—Psalm 55:17

I was quite relieved the day I discovered this verse in Psalm 55. The psalmist complained to God three times a day! Maybe it was all right for me to include complaint in my prayers.

I had always avoided prayer when my emotions were "negative": anger, fear, hurt, confusion. As a good Christian, I should be above all that, shouldn't I? But this psalm has been part of the Jewish and Christian prayer cycles for thousands of years. Evidently, no emotion is out-of-bounds when we bring ourselves to God.

So now I try to pray especially when experiencing those negative feelings. This means that God must listen to me say the same things over and over because certain frustrations and problems repeat themselves. But, like the psalmist, I believe that "he will hear my voice" in times of complaint or times of lightheartedness.

Yes, I do have a complaint, and I trust that it is safe with you,
God of heaven and earth. This is what bothers me today . . .

Generosity: Respond to Others

Why are we so reserved sometimes, too reserved to allow our feelings to show? Are we afraid others will think less of us? Are we trying to look cool?

Be generous with your emotional responses. Allow others to see your joy, your surprise, your concern, your wonder. These emotions are an integral part of your character, and when you hold back from others, hiding the way you feel, you are withdrawing a part of yourself from them.

If you're happy to see her, show it.

If his gift surprises you, show it.

If you're impressed by her accomplishment, show it.

If you're concerned about his health, show it.

Allow your emotions to touch others. They need that part of you.

Sunday

Be sure to laugh on this day of rest. Observe pets or small children at play. Ask a toddler a philosophical question and listen to the answer. Watch a favorite movie or YouTube episode that exercises your humor impulse. Exercise ordinary happiness.

Holy Spirit, please help me quiet my anxieties and fears and rest in divine presence.

Gratitude: No to Anxiety

Do not worry about anything, but in everything by prayer and
supplication with thanksgiving let your requests be made
known to God.
—Philippians 4:6

Gratitude is a high priority throughout the Scriptures. In this case, it counteracts anxiety. Anxiety loses its strength when we practice thanksgiving—remembering how God has already helped and supported us. Also, we counteract anxiety when we shift it into supplication, turning the problem over to God.

We cannot avoid emotions such as anxiety and fear. We can, however, decrease their power through prayer. Such prayer does not deny that the emotions are active; rather, it uses them to form our requests. Thanksgiving shifts our focus away from the fear about what might happen and toward the facts of what God has already done for us.

Humility: Dismiss Being Dismissed

Sometime today, another human being will glance at you and dismiss you. He or she will hardly register that you're present and will look away and forget you immediately. Or, someone will look at your shoes or hair or pants and judge you old and unfashionable or young and too flashy. This happens all the time. And that can sting—knowing for that moment that you are deemed unimportant, not worth looking at a second time.

When it happens today, dismiss the dismissal. Your identity and worth do not depend on the assessment of others. If you know who you are—God's creation, unique and with a purpose—those moments of being dismissed will not have such power to sting or discourage you.

Grow in my character the ability to stay focused on who I am rather than worry about not being better dressed, better liked, more noticed, more impressive.

Integrity: Face What You Dread

Fear and dread are great cripplers of the spirit. They can discourage us from following our callings. They can get in the way of growth and progress. They can keep us from increasing our faith, hope, and love.

Whenever you experience inner resistance, there is a reason behind it. Maybe you've taken on more than you can manage. Maybe you must learn a new skill and you're not sure you can. Maybe you've placed very high stakes on this one thing, higher stakes than it deserves. Maybe you simply haven't thought through a process, considering its possible challenges so that you can plan a strategy.

It's time to sit with yourself and ask, *What am I so afraid of? What first step can I take to break free of this fear? What help from others do I need? Why is this so critical to my self-esteem?* It's time to face the person in you who is trying to run the opposite direction, to study the look on his face and figure out what all the fuss is about.

Lord, I need the wisdom to unpack this bag of fear and dread.
Help me feel safe with you as I face this fear.

Joy: Sing a Song

In the middle of a hectic day, it can be good to drop everything long enough to sing a song. It's easy to merely listen to a song, especially if you're in the habit of turning on the radio. But it's even better to sing one—and even better to sing and dance a little dance at the same time. When you sing, you're exercising a part of yourself that doesn't get much attention, and you air out the dull, toneless self that forgets how good it is to sing and dance.

Of course, a person can't always burst into song in the middle of a board meeting. (Well, now that I think about it, would it really hurt that much?) But there's always someplace you can sneak to for a few moments to sing your little song. It can be a prayer song or a fun song or a nostalgic song or a totally-made-up-off-the-top-of-your-head song. Doesn't matter if it doesn't make much sense. It especially doesn't matter if you can't carry a tune. The real singing happens inside; the physical singing merely helps the inside voice to wake up and make some noise.

Sing for no reason at all except to take a break and give yourself a lift.

Help me sing often and with much gusto.

Openness: It's Hard to Be Happy

It's hard to be happy. There's so much standing in the way. For one thing, after every happy event, something bad is bound to happen. We all know this. We know that if we're too happy for too long, then we'll surely pay for it eventually.

So, we guard against happiness. We try to ration it out, to temper it with plenty of soberness and worry. This is a sensible, balanced way to live. Don't be too happy for too long. Then no one will notice and try to snatch that happiness from us.

What a closed-off, frightened way to live. There are no happiness quotas. Our happiness does not make God angry or anxious. God would love it if we'd just relax and enjoy ourselves.

Stop regularly—in fact, stop right now—and ask yourself what is standing in the way of feeling good this very moment. If a happy moment comes your way, embrace it. Don't let anything fill its space: no worries, no apologies, and no guilt.

May I receive whatever happiness you offer, God of love and joy.

Wisdom: Set Free

Trust in the LORD with all your heart,
and do not rely on your own insight.
In all your ways acknowledge him,
and he will make straight your paths.
—Proverbs 3:5–6

Relying on the Lord takes the pressure off of my gaps in understanding. It can be quite freeing to say, "Okay, Lord, I have no idea what's going on or what to do. I put this entire situation in your hands."

My growing reliance on God will free me emotionally to keep moving forward with gratitude and joy.

Today, God, I place this situation or part of my life in your hands, trusting that your love and wisdom will prevail . . .

Sunday

Today, try to sit with your emotions, or at least the ones you feel more prominently at this time. Allow yourself to feel exactly what you feel, but in God's loving presence.

Lord Jesus, help my whole self—body, mind, spirit—express true prayer today.

Ignatian Focus: The Physical Senses

The Christian faith has earthy roots. It began in the life of an Eastern people, the Israelites, who were nomads with their herds, then became settlers with their fields, vineyards, olive groves, and fishing boats. Jesus of Nazareth grew up shaping wood into objects for daily use, and when he embarked on a ministry of itinerant preaching and teaching, his parables, metaphors, and stories remained sharply focused on the harsh life of his listeners, as they experienced it through their senses. Fish and bread for the hungry, good wedding wine, fresh water for the thirsty, and children longing for affection and attention appealed to people's experiences of bodily and emotional need. Sometimes Jesus healed with a word, but the Gospel accounts show us a man who touched lepers, reached for the hands of the bedfast, and mixed his spit with dirt to make healing mud for the blind.

Western culture, going back to ancient Greece but persisting in our country today, has sought to separate "spiritual" people from their bodies. For centuries the body was considered a necessary evil, and Christians were expected to deny and even mortify the physical self in order to free the soul so it could thrive spiritually. We still suffer from this unnatural dichotomy. We fear and loathe our bodies in direct and indirect ways. While trying to be spiritual, we seek to quiet all physical signals because we expect them to get in the way of interior growth. Our uncomfortable relationship with human sexuality has resulted in grievous misuse of it because we have not always been able to openly and shamelessly approach our bodies as wondrous and designed by a loving God.

Our physical senses are precious gifts, and with them we can embrace our whole selves and thus love God more completely and joyfully. Through the abilities of our bodies we are able to love others, respecting their physical needs for nourishment, comfort, affection, and simple presence.

Compassion: Beyond Words

When you struggle to express compassion to someone, remember that words are not always the best resource. You can't say anything to make the situation change. Certainly your words have little impact on the feelings another person experiences when a loved one has died or some other tragedy has struck.

Now is a good time to remember the power of our physical senses:

The simple touch of your hand

A favorite song

A beautiful drawn card

A soft shawl or scarf

The scent of a candle or flowers

Homemade soup or sweets

Compassionate God, show me which sense will help me
communicate compassion today.

Courage: Feel Your Strength

To gain courage, pay attention to your body. Feel your strength when you walk or climb stairs or pick up groceries. Your body is working! It is resilient and will carry you through many years to come. You breathe in and out without even thinking about it most of the time. You can gather information through your fingertips, the soles or your feet, your eyes and ears, even your tongue.

You are a physical wonder simply because you are—you exist. Take courage from that.

Creativity: Make Room for Physical Sense

For whatever creative work you must do today, make some room for at least one physical sense. For example:

- Writing a story? Imagine not only what a scene looks like but also what scents are in the air. How does touch influence one of your characters? What sounds are in the background of a scene?

- Planning a meal? Consider the colors of the foods you will serve as well as how they will taste together.

- Arranging a room? How will the position of furniture affect acoustics? What textures do you want—a lot of soft surfaces, or smooth with angles?

Pay more attention to at least one physical sense and see what happens.

Discernment: What Does Your Body Say?

Are you making a decision today? Whether a big or small decision, your body will have its own reaction. Notice what your stomach and back feel like as you head toward one choice or another. Does your breathing change? Do you become more relaxed or more tense? How can you apply this to the process of discernment?

Jesus, you lived a human life with all its physical senses and clues. Help me pay attention to what my own body tells me as I seek to choose well.

Good Habits: Details of the Moment

One quick and simple form of meditation is a few minutes' concentration on one of your physical senses. Sit still—indoors or outdoors—and choose an object to look at; close your eyes and choose a sound to listen to (you'll soon discover you have multiple sounds to choose from); choose a texture to focus on, such as tree bark or a strand of hair or even the fur of your cat who sits on your lap; as you sit, eat a piece of fruit or vegetable and chew slowly, savoring the flavor; close your eyes and pick out a scent to focus on.

This exercise can help you slow down and become more attentive to the details of the moment.

Holy God, I acknowledge that this very moment is sacred.
Guide me as I pay attention to it.

Generosity: Sensual Gifts

When we lavish physical gifts on ourselves or others, we practice a form of generosity, and people notice and appreciate it right away. This generosity characterizes a shared meal, especially one you have prepared for others. You present them with a feast of the senses—the colors, flavors, aromas, and textures of nutrition prepared to be enjoyed.

A bouquet of flowers or any work of art speaks directly to people as physical, sensual beings. We often speak of feeding the soul, but it is just as loving to feed the physical person through gifts that stimulate and gratify the body. In this way, we honor the body as God's creation, and we cherish others as whole people.

Generous God, inspire me to be generous to others today
through the simple, sensual gifts of this life.

Sunday

Create a welcoming place for your physical self on this day of rest. Wear your comfiest clothes. Wrap up in a blanket; stretch out on the bed or sofa. Put on music you love; light a candle; make a pot of tea or coffee. Sit where the light is soft and lovely.

God of the universe, may I rest in the confidence that you uphold me with the very breath of life.

Gratitude: Thankful for Relief

Having trouble feeling grateful today? Then celebrate relief and give thanks for it:

- I was barely awake, and then I had a good cup of coffee—thank you!

- Such a cold, wet day outside, but now I'm indoors where it's warm and dry—thank you!

- After being glued to the computer all day, I watched the sun set, throwing colors across the city—thank you!

- What a horrible commute with its traffic jams and angry drivers, but look at that gorgeous Labrador retriever with his head out the back window, loving the wind—thank you!

- I ache from head to foot, from tension and lack of exercise, but I took a half-hour walk after supper, and now I'm stretched out on my comfortable bed—thank you!

Celebrate relief where you find it and give thanks.

Humility: Frail Bodies

We cannot stop the effects of time on the body. Regardless of health and fitness, organs eventually malfunction, joints wear out, and memory fades. It can be so demoralizing just going through a day and realizing how frail my body is and how limited my power is to change that.

God my creator, may this aging body serve as opportunity for me to increase my humility. I can't fool myself into thinking I'm stronger or more competent than I really am. I know I have a tendency to lie to myself and others about my own importance. Yet my body tells the truth: I'm here just a few years and then gone like a flower in the field. May this knowledge draw me closer to you.

Integrity: Grounded in Reality

One reason to pay attention to our body is that it grounds us in reality. For instance, I can spend an evening theorizing with others about how disadvantaged families need help during the winter months. It's pretty easy for a group of comfortably fed and sheltered people to make plans for bettering the world. However, when I must wait outside for a few moments and get chilled to the bone, my body reminds me of what a person feels like when he has no place to get warm. I hope that this brief experience of mine will urge me to move from talk to action in helping others.

Lord Jesus, may my discomforts guide my thoughts to the needs of others. Help me pay attention this week.

Joy: Don't Overspiritualize It

Today, don't overspiritualize joy. You might feel joy well up when you have coffee with a friend or spend ten minutes walking in sunny, gentle weather. You might experience joy when you listen to a favorite piece of music or receive a photo from a good friend. You might feel joy when you lie down to sleep after a physically exhausting day. When your body sends signals of good feeling and hope, receive them and savor them. All good gifts come from God, and we are meant to take joy in them.

Lord, may I fully appreciate this body and the physical world I live in.

Openness: Go into the Weather

I once received this advice from someone who lived in a far northern state and regularly faced brutally cold weather: Don't try to avoid the weather; go out into it. If you huddle up and simply try to stay warm and keep away the cold, you won't do anything or go anywhere. Instead, bundle up, go for walks, explore the cold outdoors, be *active* in it.

Could it be that our willingness to engage our physical environment can also cultivate an open attitude in general? If I am physically involved, opening my body to whatever the weather brings, might I become more willing to receive whatever life brings?

Try to open yourself physically to the weather. Try to open your heart to the day.

Wisdom: Down-to-Earth Stories

Jesus could have provided an abundance of "heavenly" information, given what he knew about God and the universe. He could have blessed the crowds with poetry and philosophy—after all, at just twelve years old he could debate with the Temple scribes and teachers. But he used down-to-earth stories and examples when he taught the crowd or his inner circle of disciples. He spoke of farming and animals, of building houses and searching for lost objects. He recognized that most people barely scraped by and dealt with death and illness and hunger on a regular basis. He spoke to people as physical beings who must survive a brutally physical world. His wisdom was for them, in their need.

Teach me wisdom, Jesus—wisdom that acknowledges the struggles people face—so that my words to them can comfort and encourage.

Sunday

Jesus often told stories to us. Today, tell Jesus a story about you—about your day or week or a memory or a dream.

Heavenly Father, open my heart to Sabbath rest.

Compassion: Respect Others' Experience

It's tempting to minimize or dismiss—or even become irritated by—the physical challenges of other people:

- The older relative with bad hearing
- The person walking so slowly in front of us
- The colleague who can't read the small text on the committee report
- The friend who has multiple food allergies
- The church member who has chronic pain
- The neighbor who suffers from post-traumatic stress disorder

Compassion toward such people demands that we respect their experiences and believe them when they complain. Compassion demands that we take them seriously and try to help them rather than become frustrated by their problems.

Lord Jesus, who are the people whose physical problems I have minimized or ignored, and what can I do to change that?

Courage: Living with Diminishment

It's frightening to experience diminishing physical health, to watch your abilities or those of a loved one wane and know that some of this is inevitable with age. Maybe you face the physical diminishment associated with chronic or degenerative illness. At times, it feels as if your own body is the enemy. But how can you fight yourself?

Take courage and love your physical self. Your body needs tenderness, comfort, and strengthening. Don't be afraid to work with whatever ability you still have. When your legs fail, use your arms; when your memory fails, use your wisdom, which is always with you.

Your body is still the temple of the Holy Spirit:

Do you not know that your body is a temple of the Holy Spirit within you, which you have from God, and that you are not your own? For you were bought with a price; therefore glorify God in your body.

—1 Corinthians 6:19–20

This body of yours will glorify God, even in its brokenness, in its diminishment.

I give my body to you, God, with everything that's wrong with it and with everything that's beautiful about it.

••• **THE PHYSICAL SENSES / WEEK 43** •••

Creativity: Apply the Five Senses

Choose a story from one of the Gospels and apply these instructions from St. Ignatius.

It will be profitable with the aid of the imagination to apply the five senses to the subject matter . . . in the following manner: . . . seeing in imagination the persons, and in contemplating and meditating in detail the circumstances in which they are, and then drawing some fruit from what has been seen.
—SE 121–122

"hear what they are saying, or what they might say"
"smell the infinite fragrance, and taste the infinite sweetness of the divinity."
"apply the sense of touch, for example, by embracing and kissing the place where the persons stand or are seated"
—SE 123–125

Now, talk to God about how this exercise went for you.

Discernment: Have a Good Cry

Tears happen because we need them. They offer a unique cleansing to both body and soul. Crying is a system of release that apparently is not present in any other species. Human emotion, which is connected to the deep ever-after soul, is also connected to the very pragmatic physical systems that keep out infection, regulate body temperature, fill and empty the lungs, and pump the blood. Tears are proof that we are indeed whole persons in whom the physical and spiritual merge.

We cry in response to physical pain, disappointment, frustration, anger, sadness, humor, ecstasy, and grief. Our bodies know how we feel sometimes before our brains do, and so we cry for no apparent reason—yet there is a reason. Our tears know when we've had enough already.

Don't wait for a "good reason" to cry; cry because you want to. If you want to, that probably means that you need to. Cry in private or with company. Cry naked in the shower before your day begins or bundled up on a garden bench in midwinter. Listen to your body and let the tears flow.

Good Habits: Enjoy That Glass of Water

Maybe you drink water in the morning shortly after you get out of bed. It's something you've done for years, just a habit. And yet, it helps you. After a night of sleep, your body is thirsty. You really need that glass of water. Today, drink it a little more slowly. Consider that this habit is a significant means of caring for yourself and staying healthy. Enjoy the moisture that refreshes you.

Jesus, you called yourself living water. You knew that water was crucial to life. As I enjoy having a drink of water—this mundane daily act—give me a sense of how you sustain me, physically and otherwise.

Generosity: Works of Mercy

These are what Catholics call the corporal works of mercy:

Feed the hungry.

Give drink to the thirsty.

Clothe the naked.

Shelter the homeless.

Visit the sick.

Visit the prisoner.

Bury the dead.

Corporal has to do with the physical self; corporal works of mercy tend to respond to the needs of others. Notice how physical these works are—they all involve us being physically present in being able to perform them.

We now meet many of these needs through financial donations to organizations that carry out these works on a large scale. But look at this list of seven acts and plan how to do one of them personally.

Lord Jesus, help me show your generosity by ministering to someone's physical needs.

Sunday

Do something today to put your body in motion: a walk, a stretch, some play with a child or a pet.

Holy Spirit, please guide my thoughts and meditations this day.

Gratitude: Alert to Every Sensation

In your prayer, dwell on your five senses. If the lines below don't quite fit you, write some of your own.

Thank you for colors I can see.
Thank you for birdsong I can hear.
Thank you for sunlight I can feel.
Thank you for strawberries I can taste.
Thank you for rain I can smell.
Thank you that I am not a mere spirit moving through this world.
I am a body, soft and alert to every sensation.

Humility: Bowing the Body

Bowing is a natural—perhaps, biologically speaking, innate—indication of status. I bow before the One who is greater than I am. I acknowledge before the Creator that I am the created. I am not in charge. I acquiesce to God's power over the universe.

Communicating this with my body helps me remember with my heart that God is God—and I am not.

When praying today, stand and bow at the waist. Remain in that position as you read a Scripture passage or pray for loved ones.

Integrity: What Do You See?

Mirrors are quite useful in revealing things to us. Here's a simple exercise. Look in the mirror and note the following:

- How's your posture? Are you tired, hesitant, defensive? Are you confident, relaxed, purposeful?

- What do your eyes say? Do you see fear, self-loathing, lack of sleep, anxiety? Or hopefulness, contentment, a well-rested psyche?

- Is your face a pleasant place? Do your expressions show that sheen of softness, a kind glow, a readiness to smile or laugh? Or do they carry a record of only bad events and memories?

- What does your clothing say about how you feel?

Write down your thoughts. You don't need to show them to anyone, but it's important that you make the assessment. No one else in this world will take responsibility for the story told in your mirror.

I probably look for the wrong things in that mirror. I try to see the person I'm not rather than face the person I am. Help me look with steady eyes at that person. Show me how to care for myself better.

Joy: Put on Some Music

Pull out a CD or stream some music online that lifts your soul. Take a few moments today to enjoy that music. Play it more than once if you can.

Close your eyes and listen. Does the music inspire in you scenes or words or feelings?

Can you allow yourself to smile—really smile—because of the joy this music brings you?

See how simple it can be to practice joy?

Thank you, thank you, that it's possible to experience not just relief or momentary happiness but true, deep joy simply because something is beautiful or moving or uplifting.

Openness: Breath of God

Then he said to me, "Prophesy to these bones, and say to them: O dry
bones, hear the word of the LORD. Thus says the Lord GOD to these
bones: I will cause breath to enter you, and you shall live. I will lay
sinews on you, and will cause flesh to come upon you, and cover you
with skin, and put breath in you, and you shall live; and you shall
know that I am the LORD."
—Ezekiel 37:4–6

God breathes life into us. By God's breath we come alive and
continue to live because we breathe in and out. God created our
bodies, which need oxygen—and God created the oxygen, too.

God my creator, I stand up and take a deep breath, and I feel
the air come into me. I exhale and feel it leave me. When I
breathe deeply, my body lifts and my chest opens, and I receive
the life you have given me. Your breath sustains me. I wait,
expectantly, for your breath, for my life in every moment, and
for the future you have prepared for me.

Wisdom: Listen to Your Stomach

Stomach ailments are so common that we should pay good attention to how we feel right there.

The stomach, or gut, is one of the first places our bodies register excitement, anger, stress, or fear. Our digestive system is sensitive to food, emotion, and imminent danger. Perhaps if we are careful to notice the stomach's reactions, we can grow in our awareness of how we truly feel from moment to moment.

- When a certain person enters the room, why does it feel as if my stomach is making a little knot? Do I have an unresolved conflict with this person? Why does this person set off such a reaction?

- When I choose a course of action, on impulse, why does my stomach jump? Is this my body's way of warning me that I'm moving too fast, that I should stop and think?

- When I remember an event that happened years ago, why does my stomach burn? Am I still grieving, or angry, or humiliated about what happened?

I will try to take cues from my gut today, and possibly this will lead to better self-understanding.

Sunday

Give yourself permission to do nothing in
particular, with people you enjoy.

Lord Jesus, help me go to a quiet place and find rest with you.

Ignatian Focus: Reflection

A hallmark of Ignatian spirituality is its emphasis on habitual reflection. Not only do I pray but I also reflect on the prayer afterward: How did it seem to go? At what point in the prayer did I feel especially close to God—or not close at all? Did any insight occur to me during the prayer? Do I feel called to any action because of the prayer? And so on.

Practiced regularly, reflection becomes a method of personal assessment and focus. On what do I reflect?

- A conversation or meeting
- A morning of work or play
- An action I took or witnessed
- An experience of prayer or worship
- A decision I made
- What the next step might be

By looking back on what happened, how I responded, what happened then, and what I might have learned from all this, reflection can enhance any aspect of daily life.

The Examen prayer—the daily prayer of review—is the standard form of prayerful reflection for Jesuits, and many laypeople have adopted its use. But we can look back upon any experience at any time—even years away from it—and gain understanding or healing. This is possible because we carry out the reflection prayerfully. As we reflect, we invite divine wisdom to accompany us and guide the thinking process. We allow ourselves to reexperience a moment or period of time with the faithful expectation that divine love is infused throughout the process, providing the support and insight we need.

Compassion: Memory Helps

When have you felt compassion for another? What was the situation? How were you involved? How did you feel afterward? How did compassion influence your words and actions?

Reflecting on such an experience will sharpen your awareness in future situations. We can practice Christian virtues by taking action. But we also practice them by reflecting on them, replaying them, and meditating on their impact.

Holy Spirit, I want to be more reflective about my words, actions, thoughts, and reactions. Today, help me remember an experience of compassion.

Courage: The Character You Want to Be

What's your favorite story about courage? It could be a fairy tale or crime fiction, a Bible story, a movie—whatever story impressed you because of its depiction of courage.

Allow yourself to linger with the memory of that story. What attracted you to it? Why would you describe a certain character as courageous? How has this story or character stayed with you?

Can you see yourself as the courageous character? Why, or why not?

What would it take for you to demonstrate the kind of courage you witnessed in this story? Or, if that kind of courage seems out of reach, how can you see yourself being courageous?

God, I want to have courage but need to reflect more on what it truly is. Inspire my heart today.

Creativity: A Careful Look

We're all creative, but each person's creative process is unique. Unfortunately, we don't always understand our own process. But we can learn to pay attention and become more at ease with our own creativity.

Recall a creative project you have completed in the past. It could be any form of creativity: art, writing, preparing a meal, devising a financial plan, building a shed—whatever you have done that required creativity. Now, ask yourself these questions:

- What inspired me to begin the project?
- What negative voices threatened my progress?
- What positive voices helped me stick with it?
- How did I refuel when I ran out of ideas?
- What practices or habits helped me stay on task?
- How did I celebrate when it was finished?
- How did I feel when I began? When I was in the middle of it? When the project was completed?

Write down any insight you've gleaned from the answers to these questions.

Discernment: A Discernment Postmortem

Companies often do what's called a postmortem on projects that did not go well. The team who worked on the project will systematically go back through all the steps and stages and try to identify what did or didn't work.

We can go through a similar process when our decision making has not turned out well. It helps to do this with a spiritual director or other person who can help ask the right questions, such as:

- What initiated my turning toward this decision? A conversation? An event?
- Was I motivated by strong emotion at this time? Was I trying to avoid something or someone? Was I trying to obtain something?
- Did I feel under pressure to decide quickly or to decide in a certain direction?
- Did I research the different options? If so, what did that research reveal, and how did I respond?
- Did I seek counsel? If so, how did that go?
- How did I involve prayer during this time?
- Did I pray for and wait for confirmation?

You can use similar questions to reflect on a discernment process that went well.

Good Habits: What Helps, and What Doesn't?

From time to time, it's helpful to reflect upon our spiritual practices. We can determine which practices are aiding our spiritual growth and which have ceased to be effective.

Identify the spiritual practices in your life, such as weekly worship, daily prayer, Bible reading or study (alone or in a group), meditation, and so on.

Do these practices occur on a typical schedule for you? Does that schedule seem to be working? For instance, you might read Scripture in the mornings but find that when you're running late, the reading becomes quick and without much thought. Would it be more helpful to shift Scripture reading to another time of day?

How do you experience your practices? Is there joy? Do you look forward to them? Do you experience the good effects of them during the week? Or have you begun to do some practices out of habit or mere obligation? If weekly worship has become less meaningful for you, what can you do about that? Perhaps check in with someone else in your faith community during the week to talk about the readings or the sermon or even the music.

Lord, I want my spiritual practices to have meaning and vitality. Help me make changes where necessary.

Generosity: Sit with the Memories

Try to list several ways in which people have shown generosity to you. Reflect on each situation, what happened, and how you experienced the generosity. Try to remember the details of how others gave to you and how you received from them. Sit with these memories and allow them to stir emotions and stimulate thoughts. Write down what comes to mind.

Sunday

Reflect on a favorite memory, simply for the joy of it.

May I be gentle with myself today and with the loved ones who are with me.

Gratitude: Say It Out Loud

One way to reflect on an experience is to speak about it to another person.

In fact, a beautiful form of gratitude involves reflecting on what you appreciate about someone and then expressing it to the person.

Sometime this week, reflect on what you appreciate about one of your coworkers or neighbors or family members. Then, when the time is right, tell that coworker why you are grateful for him or her. You don't have to pick out major achievements; rather, consider how this person acts every day. Perhaps she is always eager to listen to other people's ideas. Perhaps he will patiently drop what he's doing to help someone solve a problem.

This little exercise is a good practice of reflection and gratitude—for you, of course, but also for the person you thank. It's a wonderful thing to be praised simply for being yourself.

Humility: Seeing Myself Properly

When have you felt diminished lately? Or unnoticed? Or inadequate?

Spend some prayer time reflecting on these uncomfortable moments. Can you pinpoint what made you feel that way? Were the feelings of inadequacy or invisibility triggered by others' words and actions? Or were you responding to something in yourself?

Make humility the focus of your prayer:

God my creator, I want to see myself properly. I do want humility that is healthy and keeps me turning to you for what I need. I don't want my life in you to be hampered by feelings of little worth. I know you see me as one of your beloved children.

Integrity: The Moment of Clarity

Sometimes we are blessed with moments of clarity, moments when we experience true confidence in God's love for us. We also see something about ourselves that we did not see before. These moments of clarity add to our deeper understanding of who we are and how our divine purpose is unfolding.

Reflect today on who you are in God's great universe.

Remember past moments of grace that have helped establish your faith.

Joy: Formalized Reflection

It can be helpful to think of celebrations—birthdays, anniversaries, and other joyful milestones—as formalized, group reflection. We gather to concentrate our attention on a person or persons. We tell stories about a child's birth or about memorable events in a couple's years together. At such times, joy is the starting point of our reflection and remembrance.

We can practice this sort of joyful reflection on a more personal scale as well. It could be as simple as a list of people we remember in prayer. We not only pray for their needs but also call to remembrance how those people have added to our joy.

We can also mark events on the calendar and carry out private celebrations: the day the cancer treatment ended or the month we made the pilgrimage to holy sites in Ireland.

What joy will you remember today? Is it cause for celebration?

Openness: What Prepares Me?

Although we often feel as though our spiritual "condition" is unpredictable and uncontrollable, it is possible to notice what helps us do spiritual self-care.

Consider this question: What prepares me to be more open to God and others?

When have you been especially open—that is, free from fear and able to trust? Do you tend to open up to God more easily when alone or in a group? Out in nature or in a beautiful church setting? Who are the people who inspire your faith—and who are those who feed your fear?

It's surprising what you might learn simply by reflecting on what aids your soul. Try to identify one way you can better prepare for an open heart.

Wisdom: The Store Within

Each of us has a store of wisdom within. We also have memories of wisdom from others.

Write down the names of a few people who have been sources of wisdom for you.

Beside each name, write one statement that represents what you have learned from that person.

Do any of these statements resonate with you right now?

Sunday

Write down names of some of the people you love.
Then use colored pencils or pens to pray around
those names—with spirals or leaves or patterns or
starbursts of color.

God my creator, grant restorative rest to my body and
mind today.

Compassion: Memorable Image

Today I'll call to mind an image that represents compassion. Perhaps I have the image on my computer or among my photos or magazines, such as a photo accompanying a news story, or an image of a refugee receiving help or of a neglected animal finding rescue.

Perhaps I'll draw my own image of what compassion looks like.

I allow myself to remember what I've seen throughout my life, as people helped one another, as compassion overcame desperation.

Lord, help me settle on an image so that I can work with it for a while, prayerfully.

Courage: Explore the Mess

You may not think it courageous to make a mess, but often it's in the mess that we discover important information. My mess speaks to me about a task I'm confused about or items I need to be close to. Mess can tell us we're tired or discouraged or muddled and in need of decision making. Mess can indicate some aspect of my life for which I have not yet created a physical space—what does that say to me? That I should eliminate this activity or project or that it's time I spent an afternoon rearranging my home to accommodate it? Be brave and look carefully at the messiness in your life. Allow it to give you clues about what you need to do.

God, please help me look at this mess without panicking, and
help me gather important clues that can help me take one step.

Creativity: Poem Your Day

Our days can run into one another, and all seem about the same. We go to work or school, carry out household tasks, have conversations with the same people day after day. But there's always something in each day that makes it not quite the same as other days.

One way to discover what is unique about today is to "poem" the day. That is, in the middle of the day or at the end of it, come up with two or three lines that describe what happened. Create a short poem that identifies something specific about today. For example: "Lots of pink—in the morning sky / on the cover of the book I'm reading / in the cheeks of the baby on her mother's lap" or "four times I was amazed / at how many people I know / who go about life with real passion."

God, I just need a small shift in my perspective, to help me see myself and my world as new and lovely.

Discernment: Working Backward

Sometimes discernment works backward; you don't understand what God was saying until later when you review an event or a period in your life. But with God there is no past, because God is not limited by time. Everything is present tense, and this means that it's possible to mull over something that happened long ago and discern what was going on. Further, you can discern what to do with this information now that you have it.

For instance, your heart was broken by a relationship that didn't last, and you've avoided thinking about it for years because it still makes you feel like a failure. But one day you take out that memory and ask the Holy Spirit's help with it. And you can see that you gained something from the relationship, even though the ending was painful. You learned how to express yourself better to another person, or how to listen better, or how to be more honest about your own needs or more sensitive about the other person's. You understand now that your heart was trained for the better through this heartbreak, and you've adjusted the way you relate to others. If a bad memory keeps surfacing, face it squarely and let yourself be led by the Holy Spirit as you reflect on it.

Holy Spirit, thank you that it's possible to move forward now, years after an event has passed. This is a mystical part of faith that I forget about too often.

••• REFLECTION / WEEK 47 •••

Good Habits: Set Up Milestones

When your children ask in time to come, "What do those stones mean to you?" then you shall tell them that the waters of the Jordan were cut off in front of the ark of the covenant of the LORD. When it crossed over the Jordan, the waters of the Jordan were cut off. So these stones shall be to the Israelites a memorial forever.
—Joshua 4:6–7

When the Israelites crossed the Jordan River to enter Jericho, God caused the waters to pull away when the men carrying the Ark of the Covenant entered the river. So the people crossed the dry riverbed, and then they took stones from the river and erected them on the bank. This memorial would remind them of what God had done. The stones marked a major event in their journey.

Setting up milestones is a healthy spiritual practice for two reasons. One, it makes us more attentive to significant moments as they happen. Two, it helps us remember, celebrate, and give thanks for those moments, and to do so for years to come.

Your milestones might be photographs, scrapbooks, a journal, a physical bulletin board, or your social media posts and timelines. Choose a method of keeping memories that appeals to you, and try to update it regularly.

Generosity: Give Emotionally

What does it mean to be generous? Does it mean you give away a lot of money and stuff? Does it mean you volunteer for charitable organizations on a regular basis?

But what if you don't have the money to give a lot or the time to volunteer a lot? Sometimes the more difficult generosity is emotional in nature. For instance:

- Praise another's hard work, and don't worry about getting credit for what you've done.
- Allow another person to lead, when you might do it better.
- Overlook someone else's mistake or character flaw, just because you can.

This list could go on for pages. But you don't need a list. You need only one idea for giving to someone else today. What will it be?

Jesus, you know I want to be generous of heart, but sometimes I'm not too creative in this area. Show me how to be a giving person today.

Sunday

Enjoy some mindful walking today—outdoors if weather permits, or indoors if necessary. Spend ten minutes walking slowly enough to notice your surroundings. This can help you dwell deeply in your life today.

God who loves my soul, please embrace me with calm and hope.

Gratitude: When I Didn't Get What I Wanted

I remember wanting—badly—to be married, to a certain kind of man, one held in great esteem in the community where I practiced my faith. I also remember years of disappointment when that did not happen.

But, as years went by, my faith evolved, and I found myself in quite a different place in terms of theology and politics. I realized that had I gotten the "perfect" husband I wanted back in my twenties, this evolution in me never would have happened—or I would have ended up in a miserable partnership, or eventually divorced.

I can be grateful now that I did not get what I wanted. My example is rather extreme, but most of us can look back at thwarted dreams that turned out to be blessings. We watch our younger selves getting saved from our own best intentions. We're glad now that one door closed because the next one that opened was exactly the right one.

Remember a time when you did not get what you wanted but then you found what you needed. And say a prayer of thanks.

Humility: Stations of the Cross

We have, within reach, a poignant expression of humility: the stations of the cross, depictions of the fourteen events of Jesus' Passion and death. All Catholic churches have a version of the stations, and churches of the Anglican and other traditions have them as well. Many retreat centers exhibit the stations in a sanctuary or chapel, and some have outdoor installations that give you more room as you meditate and walk from station to station.

You can find numerous books of meditations on the stations of the cross and use them as you move slowly through the fourteen stations. But you don't need special materials. Simply bring yourself and the willingness to walk beside Jesus as he endures his suffering.

As you see Jesus receiving his death sentence, carrying his cross, falling under its weight three times, being stripped of his clothing and then nailed to the cross—through all these events, remember that he willingly walked among us as fully human, feeling what we feel and suffering what we suffer. He could have said no to the humiliation and the torture, but he gave up his privileges as one who was also fully divine.

Linger with the station or stations that speak to you most powerfully. Let the images speak. You don't have to say a word.

Integrity: Notice What You Say

At some point today, briefly review one or more conversations you've had in the day. Pick out one statement you made and ask yourself this simple question: Is that true?

For instance, in a conversation among friends, you agreed with someone's opinion rather than admit your questions, or you expressed a judgment of someone even though you had not witnessed any wrongdoing personally. At work, it's so easy to communicate that we're farther along on a project than we really are. In a marriage, we say that everything is fine when it really isn't.

Or, when we review our conversations, we might discover that we have in fact expressed with our words what we believe and live. These successes give us incentive to keep doing so.

Holy Spirit, make me more aware of what I say, and help me speak what I truly think, believe, and do.

Joy: Look Around!

*This is a cry of wonder accompanied by surging emotion as I pass in
review all creatures. How is it that they have permitted me to live,
and have sustained me in life! Why have the angels, though they are
the sword of God's justice, tolerated me, guarded me, and prayed for
me! Why have the saints interceded for me and asked favors for me!
And the heavens, sun, moon, stars, and the elements; the fruits, birds,
fishes, and other animals—why have they all been at my service! How
is it that the earth did not open to swallow me up.*
—SE 60

Ignatius's review of creation, and his privileged place within it,
caused him "surging emotion." He simply viewed the world
around him and pondered what it meant that he was allowed to
exist in this lavish, wondrous world that God created.

Your most direct method of stimulating joy may be this:
Look around!

*God of creation, reveal to me my life, which is cradled in this
universe you have made.*

Openness: What Triggers My Defenses?

I want to become a person who is open to God and to others. For me to develop this quality, I need to identify what causes my defenses to go up.

I look over the past few days and ask these questions:

- When did I feel threatened in any way? What caused this feeling?
- When did I feel pressed upon by others? What was happening?
- When did I feel vulnerable, uncomfortably so? What elicited this response?

Now, I reflect on these moments when my defenses were triggered and delve a bit deeper:

- Was the threat I felt a reality? If so, then I was wise to be self-protective. If not, then I can remind myself of this in future, similar circumstances.
- Were people really trying to push or press me? If so, then I was wise to establish boundaries. If not, then what can I do to build my confidence when I'm around these people?
- Was I in danger because of my vulnerability? If so, then I plan to avoid that situation in the future. If not, I pray to understand what frightened me.

Wisdom: What Went Well?

At the end of today, reflect on something that went well:

- A conversation
- A meeting
- An errand
- A time of prayer or meditation
- A task or activity

Why do you think it went well?

- Examine how you prepared or how others prepared.
- Did you pray before or during this event?
- Did you notice details of your own feelings, thoughts, or bodily reactions that helped you respond to the situation with better awareness?
- Did someone take the lead, and if so, how did that affect the outcome?

Write down one insight you've gained from this reflection.

Sunday

Sit still for a while today and focus on your body: notice every sensation, ache and pain, tension, or restlessness. Make your body—just as it is—an offering to God.

Heavenly Father, I offer my body as a temple of the Holy Spirit. Please touch me with healing, rest, and grace.

Ignatian Focus: Love

The end point for all spiritual endeavoring is love. Every prayer we pray and every discipline we learn should lead to deeper and broader love in our words, thoughts, actions, and personal traits.

The Contemplation to Attain the Love of God is a major piece in the *Spiritual Exercises*, and it is the final "set piece"; Ignatius and the other early directors of this prayer retreat understood that frail humans do not begin their formation with love fully developed. In fact, the whole of the exercises is designed to create opportunities for the retreatant to grow more open to God's love and more willing to make love his or her ultimate commitment to following God.

We usually begin to experience and comprehend God's love in the form of mercy; we become aware of our spiritual shortfall: our faults, sins, and weaknesses. When we realize that God meets us as we are and presents to us mercy, forgiveness, and healing, we are drawn into God's loving embrace. Then, as we grow in our acquaintance with the divine Person—in God the Creator, in Christ our Savior, in the Holy Spirit our helper—we are attracted to this holy communion of the Trinity and desire to be part of it. This participation involves our growing actions of holiness toward God, others, and ourselves. Our developing love and involvement draw us into the true life of God's kingdom on earth.

As we mature in our love, which we learn in our relationship to God, we come to love God simply for God's sake. Our connection ceases to be one of obligation, fear, or even holy ambition. It is a love of sheer presence.

"See what love the Father has given us, that we should be called children of God; and that is what we are. . . . For this is the message you have heard from the beginning, that we should love one another. . . . Little children, let us love, not in word or speech, but in truth and action" (1 John 3:1, 11, 18).

Compassion: Seeing a Person Differently

Love is, by nature, compassionate. Love considers how the other person experiences a situation. This facet of love is not so difficult to express to people we like and enjoy. The test of our compassion is how we interact with people who seem to be our adversaries. For instance, when dealing with a church member I perceive as overcritical of others, including myself, can I extend compassion to him? When I think this person must be miserable to be acting this way toward others, can I remind myself that overcritical people are usually hardest on themselves?

Jesus, we are all part of your body. Teach me how to act with compassion toward [blank]; help me understand how this person must feel.

Courage: Confidence in God's Love

If you have any sort of long-term relationship, then you have already discovered that true love is not for the fainthearted. When you commit to loving someone indefinitely, you sign up for a future you do not know. The person you marry will go through many changes over the years—and, in love, you will accompany your spouse through them. You love your child or sibling in the early years—his or her dependence requires it. But the child grows up and makes his own choices; the sibling does the same. The parent grows elderly and infirm. Love stays despite all of this.

For the sake of the future and your developing courage, commend your loved one to God today.

God and parent of us all, I present to you [blank], a person I love and desire to love unconditionally and for all the years we are here. You know that my love will always have its limits and frailties—it will be imperfect—yet your love envelops this relationship. You love us both with perfect love. Instill in me confidence in your love so that I will have the courage to face whatever changes and challenges come. Amen.

Creativity: Seeing the Possibility

Love believes in possibility. I remember how my grandmother imagined how I might use my talents—and she continued to dream for me when my writing life was still forming and nothing much seemed to be happening. She saw the possibilities when I couldn't.

Who can benefit from your creative vision for him or her? Whose gifts can you encourage? Whose life strategy can you inspire?

Lord Jesus, help me visualize a wonderful future for [blank],
and guide me as I encourage this person's gifts.

Discernment: The Deciding Vote

For a person of faith, love always casts the deciding vote. Whether in the mundane decisions of daily life or the larger discernments that can change the course of a life, discernment is not complete until we ask, "What's the most loving thing to do?"

This one question might make an answer immediately clear. Or, it might take us to further questions about what love is in a specific circumstance. Is it loving to protect my daughter from her own immature judgment, or is it more loving to allow her to struggle and learn and develop more mature judgment?

What decisions will you make today—about your use of time, the conversations you choose to have, the way you go about your work, the way you spend your money? Choose one decision and apply to it this question: What's the most loving thing to do?

Holy Spirit, please confirm in me the choices I have to love.

Good Habits: The Practices That Count

We can do all the spiritual formation we like, and quite diligently, but unless we form habits and practices in the overriding belief that God sees us through love, those habits and practices will become burdens, just a few more items on the schedule. If we don't believe we are already loved, we might grow to resent the prayers and meditations, the spiritual exercises and so forth.

In fact, if a spiritual practice is not forming in us a deeper and more constant sense of God's love, then we should put that practice away for a while. The point of spiritual formation is our transformation—from fearful people trapped in harmful patterns to confident people who, because they believe God loves them, become freer by the day to be who they were created to become.

What practice or habit deepens your sense of God's love for you? Do that practice with diligence, even if that means that you allow yourself to set aside other practices for now.

Generosity: Lapse in Love?

Look back on your week and identify a moment when it was hard to be generous to someone else: with your money or time, or with your praise, respect, or attention. Bring that moment to prayer:

Lord, I can tell that love was lacking in me because I held back from generosity. Forgive me this lapse in love. How could I have acted more generously in this situation?

Sunday

Praise him, sun and moon;
praise him, all you shining stars! . . .
Praise the LORD from the earth,
you sea monsters and all deeps,
fire and hail, snow and frost,
stormy wind fulfilling his command!
Mountains and all hills,
fruit trees and all cedars!
Wild animals and all cattle,
creeping things and flying birds!
Kings of the earth and all peoples,
princes and all rulers of the earth!
Young men and women alike,
old and young together!
—Psalm 148:3–12

Allow your imagination to lead you through
these verses.

Jesus, you said that Sabbath was made for humanity, not the
other way around. May I use this day for the benefit of my soul.

Gratitude: See the Day's Graces

Through the lens of gratitude, we can see the day's graces. We can recognize God's love in the day's details, however mundane.

What evidence of love have you spotted already?

What grace will you look for?

Humility: Like Christ

I desire and choose poverty with Christ poor, rather than riches; insults with Christ loaded with them, rather than honors; I desire to be accounted as worthless and a fool for Christ, rather than to be esteemed as wise and prudent in this world. So Christ was treated before me.
—SE 167

The purest form of humility is our growing desire to be like Jesus in every way:

- He was not wealthy and never sought to be wealthy.
- He was constantly misunderstood—and misrepresented—by his friends as well as his enemies.
- He was considered a fool by those who refused to learn from him and see the truth.
- He was mistreated—and, in the end, executed—because he knew who he was and would not abandon God's purpose for him.

Lord Jesus, I don't come close to being like you in the ways described here. But I am willing to become more like you as my life progresses. Please be patient with me as I learn and as my heart slowly changes.

Integrity: Born of God

Beloved, let us love one another, because love is from God; everyone who loves is born of God and knows God. Whoever does not love does not know God, for God is love.
—1 John 4:7–8

Communion with God translates into love for others. This is not theory but reality. The integrity of love cannot be compromised; its character remains constant, as does its source: "God is love."

May nothing disrupt my connection with you, God. I want your love to flow through my life to others.

Joy: Enter the Kingdom

"Come, you that are blessed by my Father, inherit the kingdom prepared for you from the foundation of the world; for I was hungry and you gave me food, I was thirsty and you gave me something to drink, I was a stranger and you welcomed me, I was naked and you gave me clothing, I was sick and you took care of me, I was in prison and you visited me."
—Matthew 25:34–36

How do I enter God's kingdom, where joy and God's blessings await me? Reach out to others in love.

I don't know if it's possible to help someone without experiencing joy at some level. Sometimes it's a visceral sensation; when I offer the simplest kind of assistance to someone, and she thanks me with true gratitude, my flesh tingles, and I can feel myself blush, not from embarrassment but from some kind of affirmation, as if my whole body understands the act of love that has just taken place.

Today, Jesus, I won't seek joy. Instead, I will look for an opportunity to care for someone.

Openness: Love As If

Love as if loving is the first thing on your to-do list.
Love as if you have no other plan but to love.
Love as if you are confident that love makes good things happen.
Love as if this is your first opportunity to love.
Love as if this is your last opportunity to love.
Love as if loving can heal all wounds.
Love as if loving is your first purpose on earth.
Love as if loving is your favorite choice.
Love as if you have that kind of power.
Love as if it will keep the earth spinning in vast, beautiful space.
—Vinita Hampton Wright, ignatianspirituality.com

Use this little poem-prayer to inspire your openness to all that God will do in your life through love.

Wisdom: Common Sense

[Jesus said,] "Is there anyone among you who, if your child asks for bread, will give a stone? Or if the child asks for a fish, will give a snake? If you then, who are evil, know how to give good gifts to your children, how much more will your Father in heaven give good things to those who ask him!"
—Matthew 7:9–11

Some wisdom is simply common sense. Jesus, who wants his listeners to trust in God's care, appeals to their common sense by posing ridiculous questions about how they treat their own children.

Yet we tend to exempt ourselves from God's love by deciding that we aren't worthy enough or faithful enough or prayerful enough. Jesus would probably ask us, "Do you stop loving your child when he makes a mistake? Do you withhold your love just because he won't listen to you?"

Create a commonsense question for yourself that will challenge your reasons for not quite believing that God loves you.

Sunday

Spend some time with this verse today.

Do not fear, for I am with you,
do not be afraid, for I am your God;
I will strengthen you, I will help you,
I will uphold you with my victorious right hand.
—Isaiah 41:10

Holy Spirit, please help me quiet my anxieties and fears and
rest in divine presence.

Compassion: Offer Forgiveness

Forgiveness is the solution to situations that have no solution. When nothing else can be done, when everything else has failed, become too complicated, and left a bad taste in your mouth, forgiveness is the step left for you to take.

Forgiveness is an act of letting go. It's required for long-term relationships, for the effective ends of wars, and for heavy-duty healing.

Forgiveness is not what you do when someone has inconvenienced you, momentarily hurt your feelings, or broken your taillight. Unless you're being really petty, you can get over those ordinary, irritating moments that visit us so often.

No, forgiveness is granted for hurt that is deep and bitter and inescapable. It's what you do when the confusion over who said or did what just keeps getting more confusing. When you can't forget about it, make up as if nothing happened, or apply all those principles of conflict resolution, all that's left is to let go and say, "I don't understand why you've done this to me, and I don't excuse it, but I forgive you."

Jesus, you demonstrated your compassion by forgiving even the people who put you to death. Give me the strength to show compassion by offering forgiveness to those who hurt me.

Courage: Love Grown Deep

It's not that I'm particularly strong or courageous.
I get tired too quickly and need much assurance,
and sometimes I eat more chocolate than is healthy.
Don't call me heroic, for heaven's sake.
But I'm invested, quite invested in the people of my life,
also the neighborhood I live in, and the country I call home.
I feel parts and pieces of myself tangled,
woven into all the living things, down to the
bright little zinnias that flourish in a front yard just south of here.
When you're that connected to the specifics of the world,
it's possible to fight hopeless battles,
to stand rooted to the spot where blood is spilled.
Courage is simply love grown deep into a stony landscape.
—adapted from Vinita Hampton Wright, *Days of Deepening Friendship*

If I have love, then I need not wonder whether I have courage. The tenacity of love is in fact a form of courage. Love stands its ground, no matter what. Love keeps giving, even into emptiness, not knowing how that emptiness will be refilled. Love carries out a task that appears to be impossible.

I would like to think of myself as courageous, but that's not really the point, is it, Lord? Show me how to love today, and I will be content.

Creativity: A New Perception

While the experience of feeling uniquely loved by God often begins in the intimacy of private prayer, it never remains private. When the person of prayer returns to his ordinary life, he recognizes and reverences God's love for him in every object, person, or event. There suddenly exists a fourth dimension in the universe—a newly found reality of God's personal love singing in the stillness and in the action of creation, in the solidity of the tree and in the fury of the thunderstorm.
—Mark E. Thibodeaux, SJ, *God's Voice Within*

Love transforms everything. It changes the way we perceive the whole world. It re-creates life as we know it. We get a sense of this when we first grow to love another person, especially if we "fall in love." Suddenly our eyes are open to the details of how this person looks or talks or walks. Everything appears wonderful to us. Or, when a baby is born, mother and father cannot stop gazing at this wonder, cannot stop touching their beautiful, perfect child. They notice and take joy in everything.

Love does not give us a deceptively positive view of life; rather, it opens our eyes to the true nature of life: glorious, lovely, filled with the breath and essence of God.

Creator of the universe, please open my eyes, through love, to see the glory and beauty of this world.

Discernment: Inner Compass

We have some equipment for our inner journey. We have the gift of discernment, our inner compass, which will show us more and more clearly and reliably where our personal true north lies—that is, in what parts of our experience, especially our prayer experience, we are most truly centered on and directed toward God. And we have our inner constellations, which show us where our clusters of desolation and consolation are most likely to be encountered. Both these gifts are given uniquely to each individual, and each of us is personally responsible to God for developing and using them, and empowered to do so by God's indwelling Spirit at our center.
—Margaret Silf, *Inner Compass*

God has designed us for spiritual navigation, what we call discernment. Love draws us toward the source of our existence, whom Jesus called our heavenly Father. We've been given the capacity to learn our interior landscape and make our way to the center, where we thrive in union with God—in communion with the Trinity: Father, Son, and Holy Spirit.

Our spiritual development is held in the Father's love. We may see a landscape that is infinite and unknowable, but all of it fits in the hand of divine love.

Heavenly Father, I accept the responsibility to learn the landscape within, to use the inner compass you've given me. Today, I'll be looking for my true north—please guide me.

Good Habits: Habits of Presence

How do I welcome people into my space, whether it's an office, kitchen, or front step?

Do I look at them directly, taking my attention off everything else?

Do I show an open posture with my body rather than folded arms or hands on hips?

Do I smile?

Do I greet them with a pleasant tone of voice?

These characteristics of friendly welcome do not come naturally for everyone. Some of us—especially those of us who tend to be intense, shy, or not very self-confident—are more likely to use closed body language and avoid meeting another's gaze. If we are preoccupied, we might not notice that our voice has a sharp tone. Depending on our mood, we may not smile at all.

Divine love constantly welcomes us with love. Jesus invites us every day to an abundant life. As his friends and followers, we extend that invitation and express welcome to others.

We can make a point of practicing eye contact, attentiveness, body language, smiles, and a welcoming voice. These are habits of presence. Choose one to focus on today as you encounter others.

Jesus, help me practice this habit of presence.

••• LOVE / WEEK 51 •••

Generosity: Give In

It feels so good to be right. But sometimes it's better to be generous.

Most of our disagreements with others are not over life-threatening issues. Most differences are simply differences of opinion. And giving in to another's opinion is one way to show love.

Here's one way to give in: "You know, you may be right. I'd rather that we get along and that you feel satisfied with the outcome. So, let's do what you prefer. How can I help you achieve what you're aiming for?"

Are you involved in a situation in which you might do the generous thing and give in? If so, how might you do that?

Sunday

Try to spend fifteen minutes in prayer today, praying, *Lord, I love [blank]*. Confess your love for as many people as you can during this short time.

Lord Jesus, help my whole self—body, mind, spirit—express true prayer today.

Gratitude: Friendship with Jesus

See the great extent of the surface of the earth, inhabited by so many different peoples, and especially to see the house and room of our Lady in the city of Nazareth in the province of Galilee. . . . [I] ask for what I desire. Here it will be to ask for an intimate knowledge of our Lord, who has become man for me, that I may love Him more and follow Him more closely.
—SE 103–104

Our desire is to grow in friendship with Jesus of Nazareth, who became a person like us, who went through this earthly existence for us, who opened the way to God's kingdom in this life and beyond.

Lord Jesus, thank you for your life, your presence, and your continuing friendship with me. Please draw me ever closer to you.

Humility: No Need for Power

If I love you, then I feel no need to have power over you.

    I don't feel threatened when you take the lead.

    I don't have to win every argument.

    I don't have to receive most of the attention.

    I don't have to prove that I'm important.

    I don't try to force you to respect me.

    I don't try to manipulate you into feeding my ego.

Love simply is not overbearing, not burdened with pride.

Humility is much lighter, much easier on the soul.

Thank you, Jesus, that you showed us what humility looks like.
Lead me on that path.

Integrity: Image of the Divine Majesty

Reflect how God dwells in creatures: in the elements giving them existence, in the plants giving them life, in the animals conferring upon them sensation, in man bestowing understanding. So He dwells in me and gives me being, life, sensation, intelligence; and makes a temple of me, since I am created in the likeness and image of the Divine Majesty.
—SE 25

You are created in "the likeness and image of the Divine Majesty." This is the ultimate truth about your existence. Claim this truth, cling to it, believe in it, wonder at it.

God my creator, you dwell in me. You give me being, life, sensation, and intelligence. You make me a temple for sacred presence. How can I not be filled with faith, hope, and love?

Joy: Look for It!

Love looks for joy.

> Love is alert to joy.
>
> Love creates joy.
>
> Love announces joy.
>
> Love expects joy.
>
> Love shares joy.
>
> What is your relationship to joy right now?
>
> What can you do today to become more focused on joy?

Even one small thing can make a big difference.

Lord, may my life become more and more joy-focused.

Openness: Take, Lord, and Receive

Take, Lord, and receive all my liberty, my memory, my understanding, and my entire will, all that I have and possess. Thou hast given all to me. To Thee, O Lord, I return it. All is Thine, dispose of it wholly according to Thy will. Give me Thy love and Thy grace, for this is sufficient for me.
—Prayer between SE 234 and 235

When, through our many experiences of prayer, meditation, silence, trouble, trial, growth, and learning, we become convinced that God's love for us is complete and eternal, we become willing to give everything we are to that love. We finally open heart, mind, will, and future to the continuous activity of this love upon our lives.

Pray the prayer above, found in the Saint Ignatius's *Spiritual Exercises*. This prayer of ultimate trust and openness is called the Suscipe.

Wisdom: Love and Understanding

To get wisdom is to love oneself;
to keep understanding is to prosper.
—Proverbs 19:8

Jesus longed to give us life—abundant life. But he could not simply hand that life to us; he taught us, told us stories, gave us the information we needed, and demonstrated how to live. In other words, he offered us wisdom: the understanding we needed to recognize the life he offered.

You and I desire to love: to love God, to love our family and friends, to love people in need, to love the world community, to love the planet on which we live. But love requires more than desire and good intentions. It requires wisdom that understands another, wisdom that pulls together memory, information, gift, and purpose. To love you, I must understand who you are and how I can best love you. To love myself, I need the wisdom that can reveal to me the false self I have created and the true self whom God loves.

God who loves me, I ask for the wisdom to know what love is
and how love acts and what love speaks.

• • • LOVE / WEEK 52 • • •

Sunday

Walk through the rooms of your house today, imagining that each room is a place in your heart. For instance, the kitchen is a place of work; the dining room or living room is a place where you welcome others; the bedroom is where your most personal desires and dreams live, and so on. Present each room to God, with a simple prayer.

God of the universe, may this room in my heart welcome you.

God of creation, may this room in my heart generate creative energy and ideas.

God who loves me, please make each room in my life a home for love.

God of the universe, may I rest in the confidence that you uphold me with the very breath of life.

About the Author

Vinita Hampton Wright is a veteran editor and writer of books and articles on Ignatian spirituality. She leads workshops and retreats on writing, creative process, and prayer. Vinita and her husband, Jim Wright, live in Chicago.

Other Books by Vinita Hampton Wright

The Soul Tells a Story

The Saint Thérèse of Lisieux Prayer Book

The Saint Teresa of Avila Prayer Book

Days of Deepening Friendship

Dwelling Places

The Art of Spiritual Writing